AF876672

For free samples, product demonstrations, and training, visit HunterDouglasContract.com/future

HunterDouglas

WINDOW COVERINGS

® is a trademark of Hunter Douglas Europe B.V.

facebook.com/workclimate

climate®

The world's first malleable workplace.

Introducing the world's first totally malleable workplace. climate® allows the individual to push and pull their space according to their work type, task, mood or even personality.

Using space more effectively means climate® gives you more options when creating your next space.

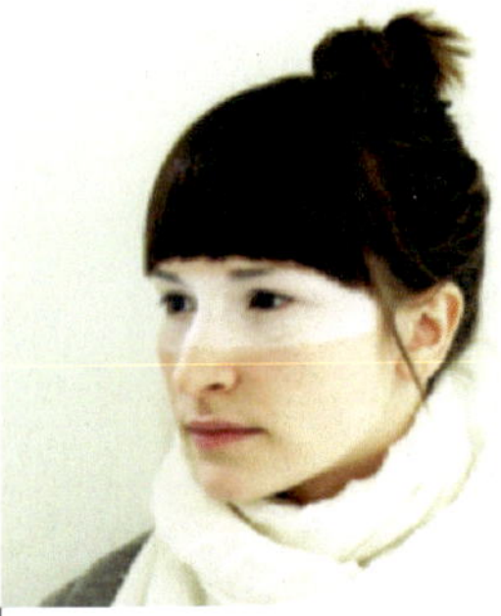

To find out more go to **http://gettag.mobi** from your smart phone, download the tag reader and scan or visit **workclimate.com**

climate®
a Schiavello initiative

PALAU
Bricks
Floyd
design - Bricks: robert bronwasser. Floyd: björn mulder
Palau | | tel. +31 (0)23 5268315 | info@palau.nl | www.palau.nl

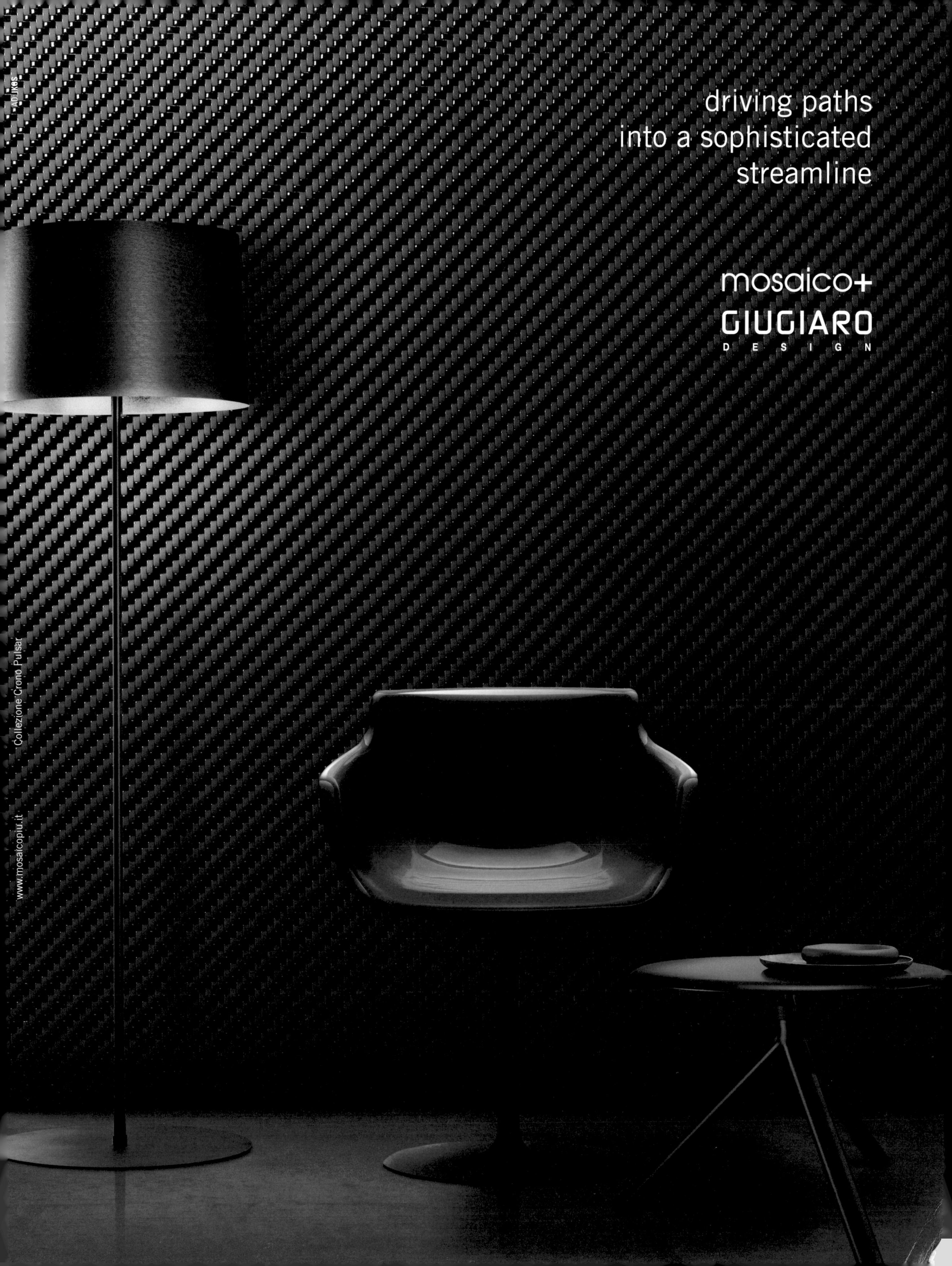
driving paths
into a sophisticated
streamline
mosaico+
GIUGIARO
DESIGN
Collezione Crono Pulsar
www.mosaicopiu.it

Urban poetry
20-24 Jan. 2012
Paris Nord Villepinte, hall 8
www.nowdesignavivre.com
International home design exhibition
Trade only.
Visitors: Promosalons
Tel : 31(0)20 462 00 20
c.rosdorff@promosalons.nl
now!
design à vivre
PARIS CAPITALE DE LA CRÉATION
MAISON &OBJET PARIS
preview, Cinna © C. Fillioux. Opinion Ciatti © Ezio Manciucca. Tacchini Italia © Andrea Ferrari. SAFI organisation, a subsidiary of Ateliers d'Art de France and Reed Expositions France.

tune the light

Midipoll LED

With Midipoll LED, ERCO presents a bollard luminaire dedicated to efficient visual comfort. Maintenance-free, compact and energy efficient, LEDs are the ideal light source for outdoor areas. Equipped with high-power LEDs in warm white or daylight white, Midipoll produces a luminous flux output of up to 420lm for a connected load of just 10W. Exclusively designed and produced by ERCO, the LED lighting technology incorporates a special prism lens to efficiently direct the light onto the target area – without glare and as such fully compliant with the Dark Sky directives. Discreet grazing light on the striking, cruciform cross-section means that Midipoll acts as a space-defining object. The sum of these properties confirms that this is where the future of outdoor lighting is to be found.

www.erco.com

ERCO

7-11 February
2012
Innovation. That is what Stockholm Furniture & Light Fair 2012 is all about. New trends, new furniture, new lamps, new materials, new know-how, new business, new contacts, new environmental and technical solutions plus much, much more. 750 exhibitors (80 % of which are from Scandinavia) will be unveiling their latest news. You don't want to miss this.
See you at the world's largest meeting place for Scandinavian furniture and light design February 7-11 2012 – welcome to Stockholmsmässan during Stockholm Design Week.
Northern Light Fair™
Stockholm Design Week
Head office. Sweden furniturefair@stockholmsmassan.se, Finland Gunilla Söderholm stockholmsmassan@lystra.fi, Denmark Johnny and Marianne Sjöberg stockholmsmassan@mail.dk, France / Belgium / The Netherlands Charles Champenois champenoisalon@hotmail.com, Germany / Switzerland / Austria Annelie Bäck-Heuser baeck-partner@t-online.de, Italy Marilena Puppi info@ogs.it, Spain Eduardo Teixeira-Alves eduardo.teixeira@prored.es, Great Britain / Ireland Jennifer Hall jennifer.hall@otsa.net
Stockholm Furniture Fair™
stockholmdesignweek.com
northernlightfair.com
stockholmfurniturefair.com
Stockholmsmässan

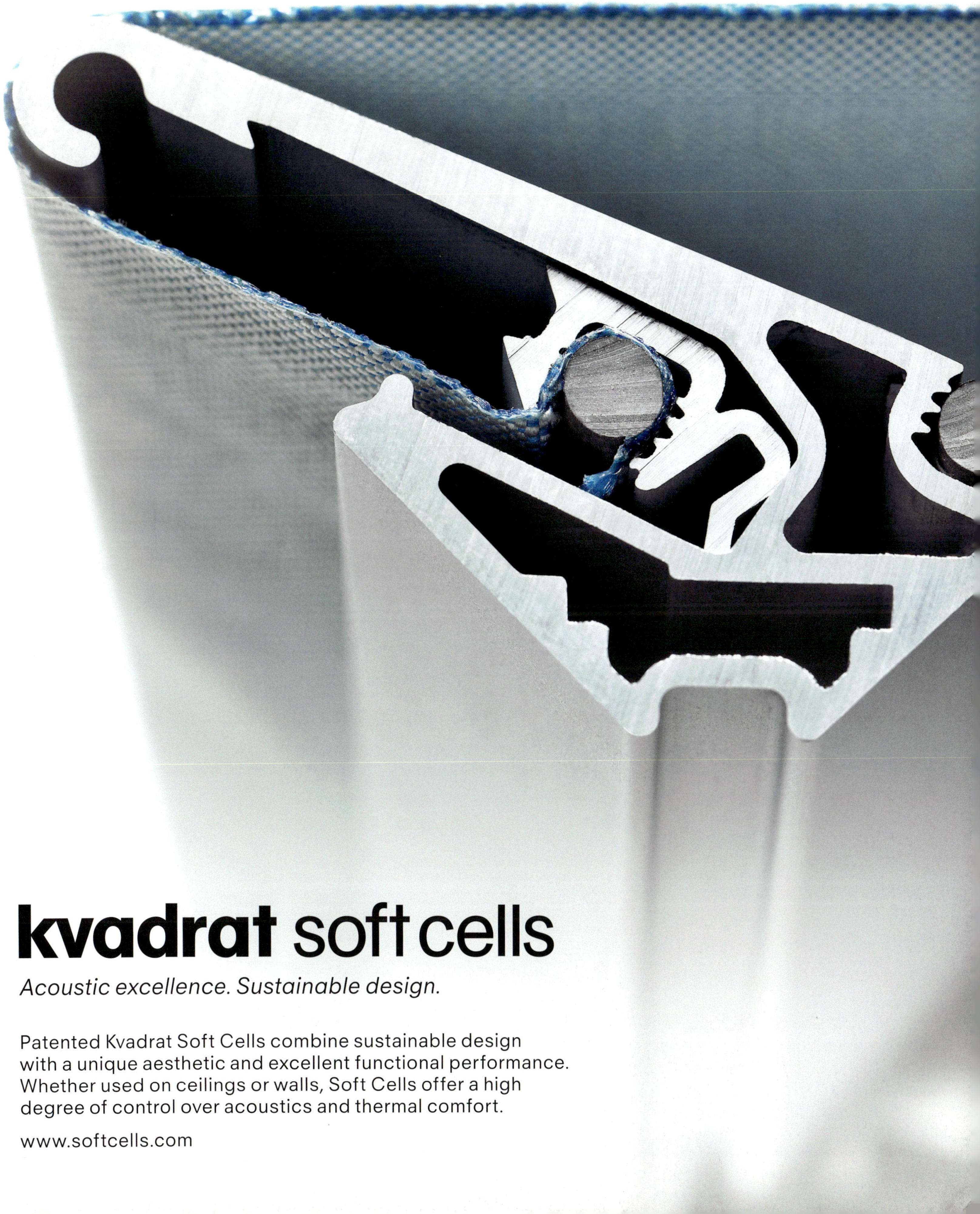

kvadrat soft cells

Acoustic excellence. Sustainable design.

Patented Kvadrat Soft Cells combine sustainable design with a unique aesthetic and excellent functional performance. Whether used on ceilings or walls, Soft Cells offer a high degree of control over acoustics and thermal comfort.

www.softcells.com

One of a kind

Introducing the world's first quartz collection
with a unique pattern on each slab.
Supremo, the exclusive one-of-a-kind collection.

caesarstone®
Supremo™

Available at selected showrooms and dealers www.caesarstone.com

Available on the App Store

Evolution Communication is the basis for continued growth – USM expands ideas to open up possibilities.

Visit our showroom or request detailed information.

International: USM U. Schärer Söhne AG, 3110 Münsingen Switzerland, Phone +41 31 720 72 72
USA: USM U. Schaerer Sons Inc., 28–30 Greene St., New York, NY 10013, Phone +1 212 371 1230
Showrooms: Berlin, Bern, Düsseldorf, Hamburg, New York, Paris, Tokyo
info@usm.com, www.usm.com

USM
Modular Furniture

HANS BOODT.
CREATING
CHARACTERS

WWW.HANSBOODT.COM

Contents

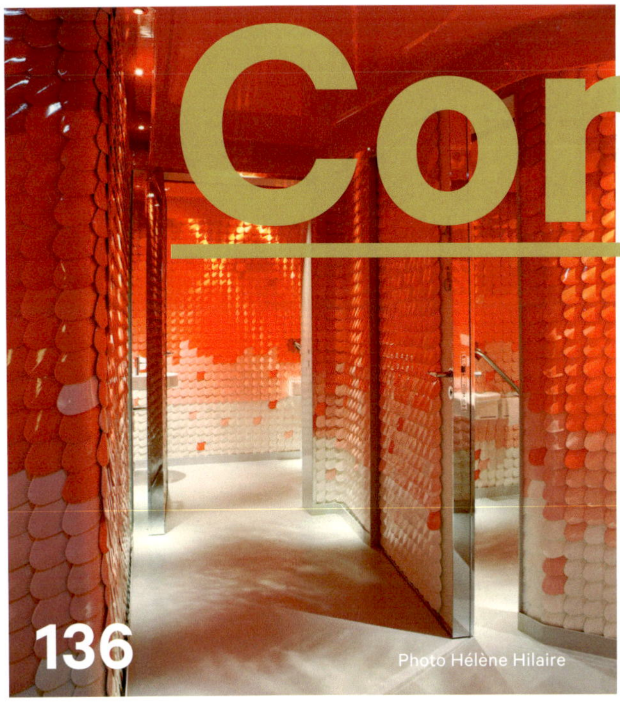

Photo Hélène Hilaire

Features

Photo Takumi Ota

Photo Jun Nakamichi (Nacása & Partners)

Visions

Photo Sergio Pirrone

Stills

Photo Roland Halbe

Reports

Goods

heimtextil

11 – 14. 1. 2012
www.heimtextil-trends.com

messe frankfurt

Frame
Laan der Hesperiden 68
NL-1076 DX Amsterdam
T +31 20 423 3717
F +31 20 428 0653
info@framemag.com
framemag.com

Editorial
editorial@framemag.com

Editor in chief
Robert Thiemann

Managing editor
Femke de Wild

Editors
Tracey Ingram
Jane Szita

Editorial intern
Onilee Zaborniak

Contributing editors
Shonquis Moreno
Alexandra Onderwater
Louise Schouwenberg
Chris Scott
Michael Webb

Copy editor
Donna de Vries-Hermansader

Graphic design
Mariëlle van Genderen
Cathelijn Kruunenberg
Adriaan Mellegers

Graphic design intern
Barbara Iwanicka

Translation
InOtherWords (Donna de Vries-Hermansader)

Contributors to this issue
Yoko Choy
Penny Craswell
Giovanna Dunmall
Matt Flemming
Grant Gibson
Carlos M Guimarães
Kanae Hasegawa
Jeroen Junte
Cathelijne Nuijsink
Anna Sansom
Masaaki Takahashi
Katya Tylevich
Charlotte Vaudrey
Suzanne Wales

Web editor
Lydia Parafianowicz
lydia@framemag.com

Cover
Photo Hélène Hilaire

Lithography
Edward de Nijs

Printing
Grafisch Bedrijf Tuijtel
Hardinxveld-Giessendam

Paper
300gr Matterhorn, 135gr Sappi Mat, 115gr Hello Gloss and 100gr IJsselprint

Publisher
Peter Huiberts
peter@framemag.com

Distribution
Benjamin Verheijden
benjamin@framemag.com

Finance
Sandy Kenswil
sandy@framemag.com

Advertising
Elles Middeljans
elles@framemag.com

Nienke van der Maar
nienke@framemag.com

Online advertising
Nikki Brandenburg
nikki@framemag.com

Advertising representatives
Austria/Germany/Switzerland
Wolfram Werbung
Xenia Lange
Feringastrasse 9a
D-85774 Unterfoehring
T +49 89 992 493 990
F +49 89 992 493 999
wolframwerbung.com
lange@wolframwerbung.com
wolfram@wolframwerbung.com

Italy
Studio Mitos
Michele Tosato
Via Valdrigo 40
I-31048 San Biagio di Callalta (TV)
T +39 0422 894 868
F +39 0422 895 634
studio.mitos@tin.it

Spain
Caplin Communications
Vibeke Gilland
C/. San Rafael, 21
E-28244 Pozuelo de Alarcón
Madrid
T +34 91277 5312
M +34 655 189 585
vibeke.gilland@caplincommunications.es

United Kingdom
Francine Libessart
T +44 20 7704 0944
francine@framemag.com

License holders
China
Frame China
Jacky Liu Zhanhui
T +86 411 8437 6131
jackyl@archi-china.com

Korea
TYM Co., Ltd.
Young Lee
T +82 8169 6013
info@tym.co.kr

Russia
Mediacrat
Alexei Medvedev
T +7 495 627 7841
info@mediacrat.eu

Turkey
Tasarim Publishing Group Ltd.
Enis Tibet
T +90 21 2296 6758
info@framedergisi.com

Subscriptions
subscriptions@framemag.com
framemag.com

Subscription representatives
Japan
Memex Inc.
4-9-8 Minamisenba,
Chuo-ku
JP-542-0081 Osaka
T +81 6 6281 2828
F +81 6 6258 4440
info@memex.ne.jp
memex.ne.jp

Korea
TYM Co., Ltd.
B-dong 2FL, 271-3
Ahyun-2dong
Mapo-gu
Seoul 121-859
T +82 8169 6013
info@tym.co.kr

Singapore
Basheer Graphic Books
Block 231 Bain Street #04-19,
Bras Basah Complex
SG-180231 Singapore
T +65 6336 0810
F +65 6334 1950
bgbooks@singnet.com.sg

Subscription rates
1-year €95
2-year €180
1-year student €85
2-year student €160

How to subscribe?
Visit framemag.com or telephone +31 20 423 3717.

FRAME (USPS No: 019-372) is published bimonthly by FRAME Publishers and distributed in the USA by DSW, 75 Aberdeen Road, Emigsville, PA 17318. Periodicals postage paid at Emigsville, PA. POSTMASTER: send address changes to FRAME, c/o PO Box 437, Emigsville, PA 17318-0437.

Bookstore distributors
Australia
Speedimpex Australia Pty Ltd
T +61 2 9371 8866
F +61 2 9371 8867
sales@selectair.com.au

Austria
Morawa Pressevertrieb
T +43 1 5156 2190
F +43 1 5156 2881 955
mbaburek@morawa.com

Belgium
IMAPress
T +32 14 423 838
F +32 14 423 163
info@imapress.be

Exhibitions International
T +32 16 296 900
F +32 16 296 129
info@exhibitionsinternational.be

Brazil
Livraria Freebook
T +55 11 3256 0577
F +55 11 3259 1120
info@freebook.com.br

Canada
LMPI
T +1 514 355 5674
mcoutu@lmpi.com

China
Frame China
Jacky Liu Zhanhui
T +86 411 8437 6131
jackyl@archi-china.com

Cyprus
Nasis Ltd.
T +357 9624 3125
niki@nasisbooks.com

Denmark
Interpress Danmark
T +45 3327 7744
F +45 3327 7701
rr@interpressdanmark.dk

Dubai
Tawseel Distribution
T +971 4344 2222
info@tawseel.com

Finland
Akateeminen Kirjakauppa
T +358 9 121 4330
F +358 9 121 4241
juha.kaski@stockmann.fi

France
OFR Systems International
T +33 1 4245 7288
F +33 1 4018 3978
info@ofrpublications.com

Germany
IPS Pressevertrieb
T +49 2225 8801 182
F +49 2225 8801 59182
lstulin@ips-d.de

Vice Versa Vertrieb
T +49 3061 6092 36
F +49 3061 6092 38
info@vice-versa-vertrieb.de

Greece
Papasotiriou Bookstores
T +30 10 332 3306
F +30 10 384 8254
diamantopoulos@papasotiriou.gr

Hong Kong
The Grand Commercial Co., Ltd.
T +852 2 570 9639
F +852 2 570 4665
thegrandcc@i-cable.com

Hungary
IPS Pressevertrieb
T +49 2225 8801 182
F +49 2225 8801 59182
lstulin@ips-d.de

India
SBD Subscription Services
T +91 11 2871 4138
F +91 11 2871 2268
sbds@bol.net.in

Indonesia
Basheer Graphic Books
T +62 21 720 9151
F +62 21 720 9151
info@basheergraphic.com

Italy
Idea Books SRL
T +39 0445 576 574
F +39 0445 577 764
info@ideabooks.it

Japan
Memex
T +81 6 6281 2828
F +81 6 6258 4440
info@memex.ne.jp

Korea
TYM Co., Ltd.
T +82 70 8169 6013
F +82 2 364 1341
info@tym.co.kr

Malaysia
Basheer Graphic Books
T +603 2713 2236
F +603 2143 2236
info@basheergraphic.com

Malta
Miller Distributors Ltd.
T +356 2166 4488
info@millermalta.com

Middle East
AA Studio
T +961 1 990 199
F +961 1 990 188
aastudio@inco.com.lb

Netherlands
Betapress
T +31 16 145 7800
F +31 16 145 3161
m.maican@betapress.audax.nl

New Zealand
Mag Nation Auckland
T +64 9366 6216
info@magnation.com

Norway
Listo AB
T +46 8 792 4668
carola.genas@listo.se

Poland
IPS Pressevertrieb
T +49 2225 8801 182
F +49 2225 8801 59182
lstulin@ips-d.de

Portugal
International News Portugal
T +351 21 898 2010
mario.dias@internews.com.pt

Tema
T +351 21 342 4082
F +351 21 716 6925
belmiro@mail.telepac.pt

Russia
Mediacrat
T +7 49 5228 4919
arman@mediacrat.ru

Serbia/Macedonia/Bosnia & Herzegovina/Montenegro
ARBOOKS d.o.o Beograd
T/F +381 11 242 7183
office@arbooks.net

Singapore
Basheer Graphic Books
T +65 336 0810
F +65 334 1950
info@basheergraphic.com

Slovakia
Art Books s.r.o.
T +421 25 2494 919
info@artbooks.sk

South Africa
Magscene
T +27 11 579 2000
F +27 11 579 2080
info@magscene.co.za

Spain
Promotora de Prensa Internacional SA
T +34 93 245 1464
F +34 93 265 4883
evelazquez@promopress.es

Sweden
Svenska Interpress AB
T +46 8 5065 0615
F +46 8 5065 0750
susanne.pettersson@interpress.se

Switzerland
IPS Pressevertrieb
T +49 2225 8801 182
F +49 2225 8801 59182
lstulin@ips-d.de

Taiwan
Long Sea
T +886 2 2706 6838
F +886 2 2706 6109
eric@longsea.com.tw

Turkey
Tasarim Publishing Group Ltd.
T +90 21 2296 6758
info@framedergisi.com

United Kingdom
Comag
T +44 20 1895 4337 33
F +44 20 1895 4336 03
bill.palmer@comag.co.uk

USA
Ubiquity Distributors
T +1 718 875 5491
F +1 718 875 8047
info@ubiquitymags.com

Comag
T +44 20 1895 4337 33
F +44 20 1895 4336 03
bill.palmer@comag.co.uk

Consortium Book Sales & Distribution
T +1 800 283 3572
F +1 612 746 2600
info@cbsd.com

a new vision: Kelvin LED
design by Antonio Citterio with Toan Nguyen
FLOS
www.flos.com

Worktop LYRA / Sink INTEGRITY

SILESTONE 10 YEARS WARRANTY
RESISTANCE TO SCRATCHING
RESISTANCE TO ACIDS
SILESTONE PREMIUM
RESISTANCE TO STAINING
WIDE RANGE OF COLOURS

Fernando Alonso for Silestone®

An 'authentic' life is within us all; with each decision, with each experience. We aspire to feel 'authentic'.

Silestone® makes it possible to express our true selves throughout the home. The only worktop with bacteriostatic protection, and available in different textures.

Live the authentic life, live your life with Silestone® www.silestone.com

SILESTONE® by COSENTINO

THE ORIGINAL

SWIVEL CHAIR CORPO
BURKHARD VOGTHERR, DESIGNER:
“I USED INTERWOVEN ELASTIC BELTS FOR THE BACKREST. – IT LOOKS ELEGANT AND IS VERY COMFORTABLE.”

www.girsberger.com/004

girsberger

susanne-kreuzer.com

IDS12
Interior
Design
Show

January
26 to 29
2012
Toronto

IDS12
Canada's
Largest
Contemporary
Design Fair

Metro Toronto
Convention Centre

Ideas.
Inspiration.
Details.
Culture.
Party.

01.26	01.27	01.28	01.29
Opening Night Party	Professional Trade Day	General Admission	General Admission

Register Today at
InteriorDesignShow.com

Title Sponsor
RADO
SWITZERLAND

IDSToronto
@IDSToronto

PRODUCED BY MMPI
CANADA

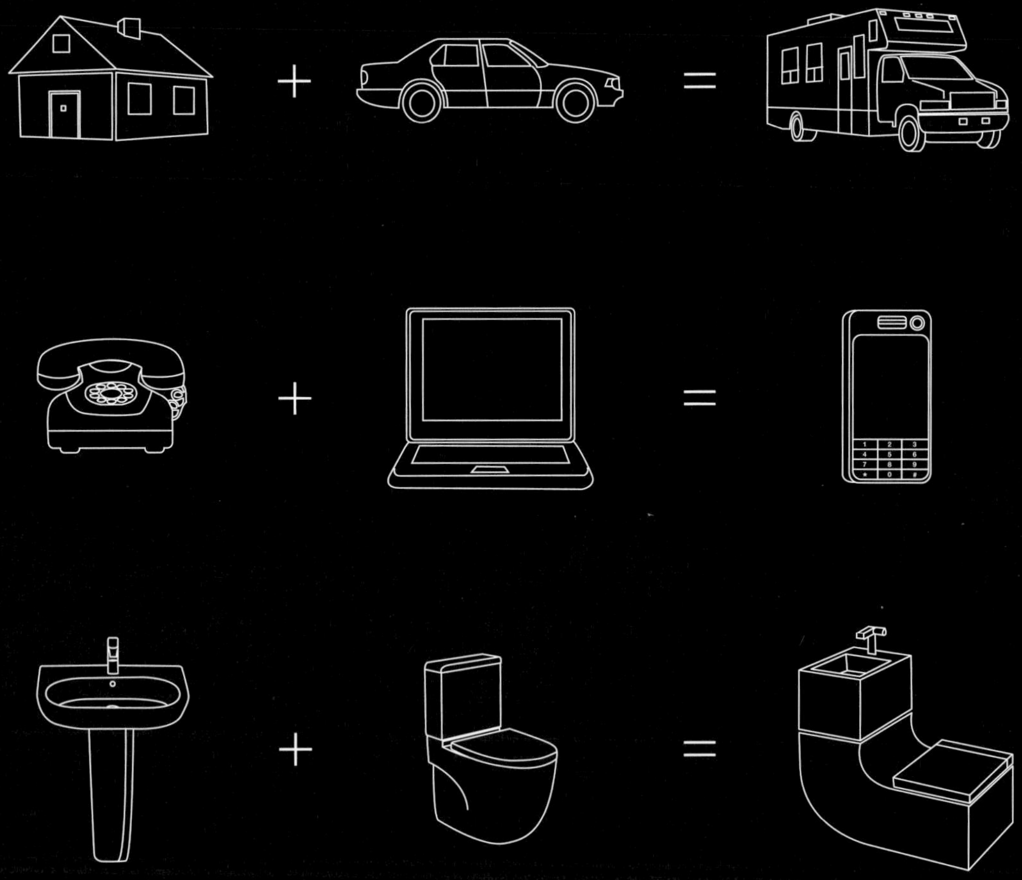

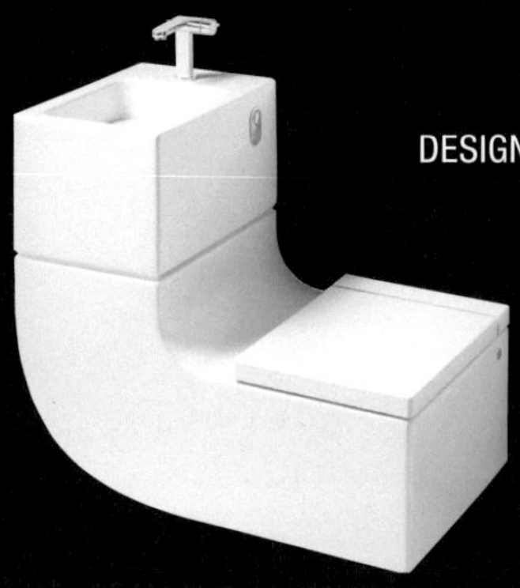

DESIGN + SUSTAINABILITY = W + W

W+W has arisen from Roca's ambition upon incorporating new, unique and innovative solutions into bathrooms. This solution combines design and sustainability as it brings the toilet together with the washbasin in a single piece. An eye-catching design makes it ideal for compact spaces, although its most innovative feature is technology that allows water from the washbasin to be reused to fill the toilet's cistern. A unique product that Roca has made a reality.

Roca

THE LEADING GLOBAL
BATHROOM BRAND
www.roca.com

VISION
FASHION MANNEQUINS
visionmanichini.it
HOGAN
HOGAN

We're enhancing the beauty and comfort of homes on the inside—and kerb appeal on the outside.

PPG has been right at home with leading designers and architects for years. Our coatings let them design exteriors that stand up to the elements and stay looking great, and interiors that reflect the perfect mood and style. PPG's architectural coatings include everything from low-VOC paints and stains to self-cleaning exterior coatings and a full range of performance coatings products. And, PPG helps clients translate emerging global colour trends and simplify colour selection with innovative tools. From architectural coatings to consumer products, automotive to aerospace, marine and industrial applications, we're bringing innovation to the surface. Visit **ppg.com** to learn more.

SIGMA COATINGS

A brand of PPG

PPG Industries

Bringing innovation to the surface.™

PAINTS - COATINGS - OPTICAL PRODUCTS - SILICAS - CHEMICALS - GLASS - FIBRE GLASS

"Bringing innovation to the surface." is a trademark of PPG Industries Ohio, Inc.

Nebel
New catalogue out now!
Order your free copy via www.deltalight.com
The Nebel lighting object succeeds effortlessly in putting the observer on the wrong foot with its surprising volume. Everywhere this eye-catcher is given space it opens up a game of stylised forms and warm light.
DELTALIGHT®

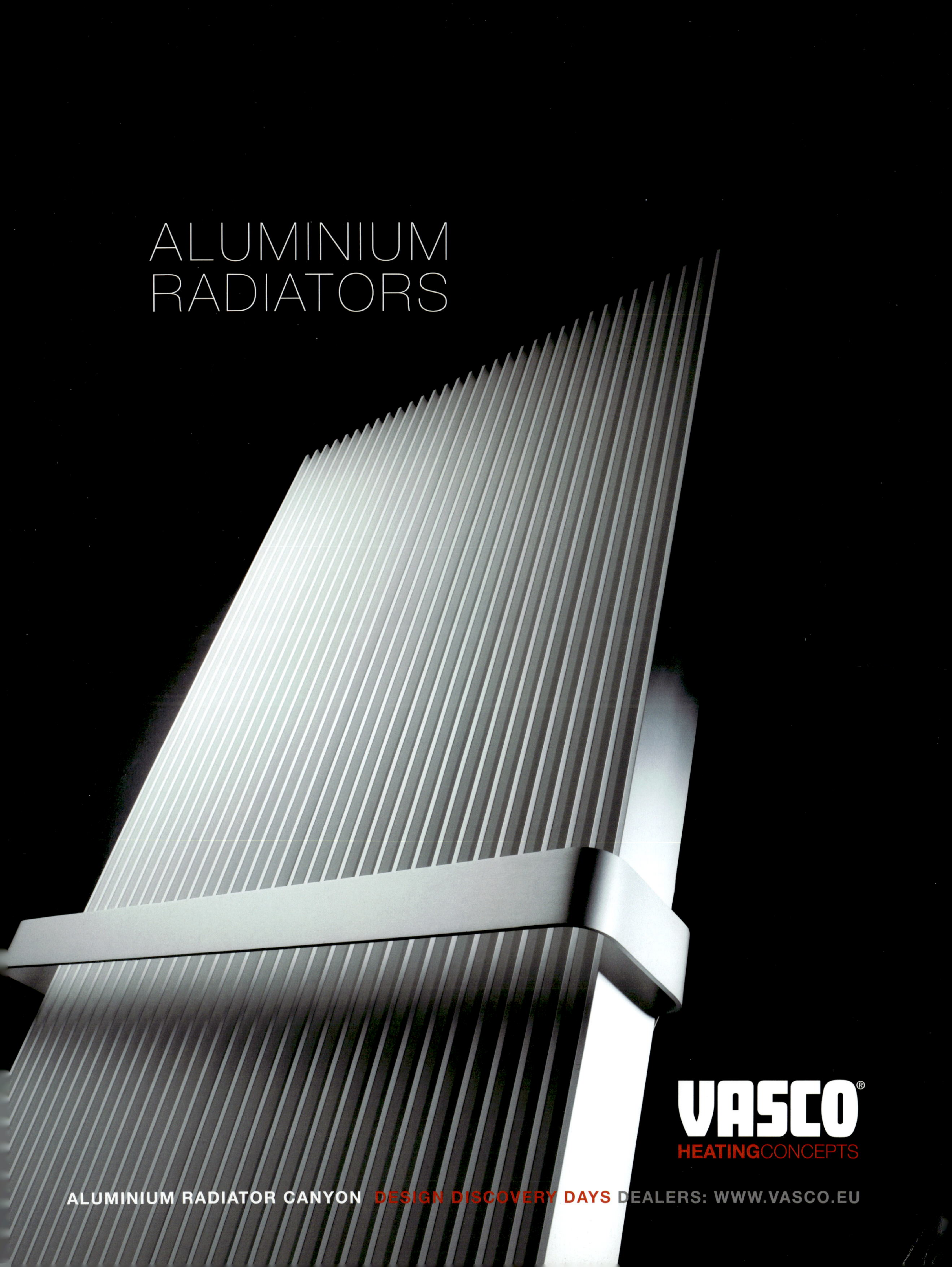
ALUMINIUM
RADIATORS
VASCO®
HEATINGCONCEPTS
ALUMINIUM RADIATOR CANYON DESIGN DISCOVERY DAYS DEALERS: WWW.VASCO.EU

Visions

Pegan Petkovšek
by Enota

Part of a comprehensive renovation of Svoboda Sports Park, Slovenia's National Gymnastics Centre provides uninterrupted views of training areas.
Competition entry
Ljubljana, Slovenia
enota.si

The expansion eliminates the need for traditional theatres

Cineteca Nacional del Siglo XXI
by Rojkind

The expansion of Mexico's national film archive is based on promoting communication between users as a way of eliminating the need for traditional theatres.
Expected completion 2012
Mexico City, Mexico
rojkindarquitectos.com

The Canopy
by NEXT and Mass Studies

A student pavilion at Erasmus University in Rotterdam works in harmony with the canopy of surrounding trees.
Competition entry
Rotterdam, the Netherlands

nextarchitects.com
massstudies.com

Sinfonia Varsovia
by Atelier Thomas Pucher

The design of the new Sinfonia Varsovia includes an 1800-seat auditorium, rehearsal rooms, music workshops and a small hotel for artists in residence and vacationing music lovers.
Winning competition entry
Expected completion 2016
Warsaw, Poland

thomaspucher.com

Uncommon Creatures
by Anne-Mette Krolmark

Anne-Mette Krolmark merges the dark world of Danish menswear label Uncommon Creatures with an exhibition on overconsumption and mass production.
Student work
New York, New York, USA

krolmark.dk

Serlachius Museum Gösta Extension
by FRAMA and Juliane Demel

A central 'heart' unites the wings of a sprawling 4700-m^2 museum building whose design connects the complex with its picturesque environment.
Competition entry
Mänttä, Finland
frama-architekten.de
julianedemel.de

Visualizations Anikó Krén

Shoppers traverse the game terrain

Above Ground Rebel Bingo
by JSPY

A 'bingo platform' featuring the components of an apartment is JSPY's concept for a pop-up store in which shoppers traverse the game terrain.
Competition entry
New York, New York, USA
jspyarchitecture.com

UEL Docklands Entrance Pavilion
by Surface

Tilted, blue-metal structures frame the entrance of a reception and security pavilion, while expressing the distinction between internal and external pedestrian routes.
London, England, UK
surfacearchitects.com

BRANDVAN
® EGMOND

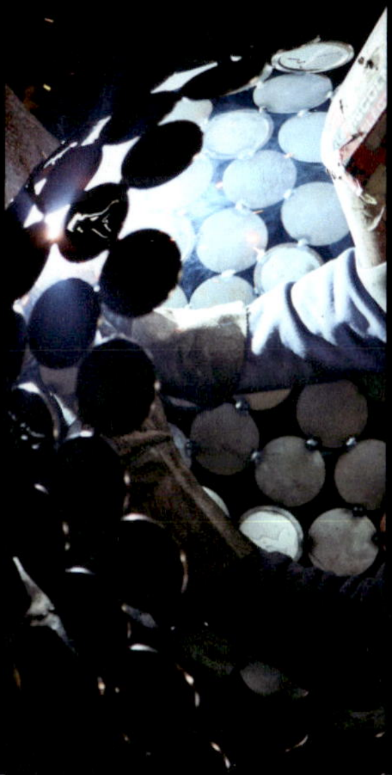

Welcome to the world of BRAND VAN EGMOND

BRAND VAN EGMOND is a well-known Dutch 'Haute Couture' Lighting label. For more than 22 years, founder William Brand and Annet van Egmond have been responsible for the concept, design and art-direction of the brand.
This year, the team was honoured to design a lighting sculpture for today's world leader in luxury craftsmanship, LOUIS VUITTON, for their latest store in Las Vegas. The innovative design studio of **BRAND VAN EGMOND** is based in the Netherlands, where a team of designers creates its custom-made objects. Following intensive cooperation with other architects and designers, **BRAND VAN EGMOND®** crafts the exclusive results in its workshops. In November 2011, the stunningly renovated showroom and design studio will be ready for more action.

www.brandvanegmond.com

Taittogami
by Matteo Cainer

Origami techniques such as layering and folding become architectural elements in a proposal for an extension of Serlachius Museum Gösta.
Competition entry
Mänttä, Finland

matteocainer.com

Roundel Pavilion
by Joseph Sung

An information pavilion for the 2012 Olympic Games pays homage to the red, white and blue London Underground roundel that is synonymous with the UK's capital city.
Competition entry
London, England, UK

vonsung.com

Pulsen Community Centre
by SEA and Elkiær + Ebbeskov

Designed to reinvigorate rural living, Pulsen is a village within a village comprising a sports centre, healthcare facilities and cultural spaces.
Winning competition entry
Expected completion 2013
Balling, Denmark

s-e-a.dk
ee-arkitekter.dk

Staircases encased within glass form the basis of an urban theatre

The Living Museum
by Emma McEwen

Staircases encased within glass form the basis of an unconventional inner-city theatre inspired by Antonin Artaud's 'Theatre of Cruelty'.
Student work
Auckland, New Zealand

MASTER MEUBEL TURNHOUT

MARALUNGA by Vico Magistretti and Cassina. Design first.

MASTER MEUBEL - STEENWEG OP DIEST 111 - 2300 TURNHOUT - +32(0)14/416113

MASTER

W W W . M A S T E R M E U B E L . B E

Cassina

WWW.IMM-COLOGNE.COM
imm
Living Interiors
The event for bathrooms, flooring, wallcoverings, lighting at imm cologne.
imm cologne
CREATE. FURNISH. LIVE.
THE INTERNATIONAL FURNISHING SHOW
16 – 22.01.2012
koelnmesse
Koelnmesse GmbH, Messeplatz 1, 50679 Köln, Germany, Tel. +49 180 5 91 3131, Fax +49 221 821-99 1180, imm@visitor.koelnmesse.de

Ph. Leo Torri

Sedetevi sugli allori.

PREMIO
COMPASSO D'ORO ADI

Frida, design Odoardo Fioravanti. XXII Premio Compasso d'Oro ADI.

PEDRALI®

pedrali.it

Architect:
DESIGN INTERNATIONAL
London - UK
www.designinternational.com

Developer:
TRIGRANIT
Developement Corporation

Contractor:
MUCIC & Co.

Project:
ARENA CENTAR
Zagreb - CRO
www.arenacentar.hr

MIRAGE provides the ideal solution to modern architectural needs.

A library of coordinated wall and floor coverings, ventilated facades, floating floors, swimming pools, gardens and tactile flooring: **Mirage is the perfect partner** for cutting-edge technology and uncompromised elegance.

www.mirage.it

MIRAGE
close to your inspiration

New Developments in 2011: AirPad, the new office swivel chair with the totally unique transparent membrane shows its true colours, as a masterpiece of aesthetic architecture and the next stage in the evolution of design and backrest ergonomics. Volume 8, the new vision in office seating, which feels just as at home in the living room as in the office environment. Try them out in the interstuhl Arena or at www.airpad-chair.net.

Interstuhl Büromöbel GmbH & Co. KG · Brühlstr. 21 · D 72469 Meßstetten-Tieringen · Phone +49 7436 871-0 · www.interstuhl.com

interstuhl

Where there's an AirPad, there's transparency and beauty

Microsoft Visitor Center

Woven wire fabric from Cascade Coil

Projects include multi-story wire mesh draperies for hotels, auditoriums, and casinos; curved dividers for visual merchandising; window treatments for private homes; safety screening for industrial settings; sculptural forms for urban gardens; decorative interior/exterior wall coverings for buildings and parking garages; aviary round weave screening for animal habitats, and see-through appealing barriers for commercial security. Whatever the application, let us help you realize your creative vision.

www.cascadecoil.com | **T+1.971.224.2188**

dive
Design Kati Meyer-Brühl

brühl
www.bruehl.com
brühl & sippold · Postfach · D-95138 Bad Steben oder Fax +49 (0)9288/95599 · info@bruehl.com

Stills

068
Air Play
Ryo Yamada

Photo Neil Hartman

Photo Daici Ano

074
Branching Out
Hironaka Ogawa

Photo Martine Houghton

052
Diamond Cuts
Maison Martin Margiela

Odile Decq's red carpet moment

Words **Chris Scott**
Photos **Roland Halbe**

Built in 1875 by Charles Garnier, the Opéra de Paris Garnier is one of the city's more spectacular functioning monuments. Although Garnier initially envisaged a restaurant in the Rotonde du Glacier, we had to wait 136 years before architect Odile Decq created one. Bringing a distinctive flair and style to her projects, the passionate designer likes to push the envelope. Despite the restrictions that come with working in a listed building – it was impossible to touch walls, columns or vaulted ceilings – Decq succeeded in giving the historic environment a fresh, strong, contemporary look.

Among the existing elements she created an undulating, completely transparent glass façade that is supported by a metal structure held in place by brackets – all hovering some 6 m above the floor. The organically shaped mezzanine, completely free of the walls, has legs that conceal all necessary mechanical systems, a subtle reference to the original opera. Chairs manufactured by Poltrona Frau and tables in Corian are also Decq designs.

Red dominates the dining room. Calling it 'my signature', Odile says that 'you find red in all my projects; it's a colour that evokes life'. Her futuristic restaurant interior is a theatrical solution that seems to have glided into the vaulted space with smooth precision.

odbc-paris.com

Odile Decq designed a theatrical, highly contemporary, freestanding structure for a restaurant that complements listed monument Opéra de Paris Garnier.

"THE BEST FRIEND ON EARTH OF MAN IS THE TREE.
WHEN WE USE THE TREE RESPECTFULLY AND ECONOMICALLY,
WE HAVE ONE OF THE GREATEST RESOURCES ON THE EARTH."
- Frank Lloyd Wright
American White Oak Deeply smoked - Suitable for underfloor heating
ebonyandco
handcrafted solid wood floors
www.ebonyandco.com
Amsterdam Herengracht 516 1017CC +31 (0)20 616 3444 amsterdam@ebonyandco.com
Worldwide Showrooms New York Dublin London Amsterdam Moscow Barcelona

A spoonful of sugar from Bluarch

The interior of Omonia Café in New York evokes the delectable delights on display.

Words **Shonquis Moreno**
Photos **Scott G. Morris**

Ever wanted to just get it over with and tuck yourself into a pastry, instead of tucking the pastry into you? Now you can do both. In the unlikely but growing design hotspot of New York's Astoria, Queens, Bluarch's Antonio Di Oronzo has cooked up the Omonia café, an oozing 93-m^2 bakery with luscious textures that evoke the sensuous pleasure of, say, a profiterole. The ceiling melts into side walls, forming a single surface glazed to varying heights with bite-size chocolate-brown Bisazza tiles, while 15-cm tubular incandescent bulbs peek from behind a drop ceiling of multiple pendulous, red-cedar spheres.

Exposed in a tempered-glass box, the kitchen's careful construction matches the refinement of the handcrafted pastries. 'We wanted the space to exist at two scales of perception,' explains Di Oronzo, who has designed award-winning nightclubs and restaurants but never a bakery. 'The first layer had to be within the realm of the actual pastries, while the second materialized in the bigger gesture of the shifting and bubbling tiled surface.'

bluarch.com

Facet Studio sneaks a peak in Sydney

Words **Tracey Ingram**
Photo **Katherine Lu**

With almost 300 shoes to display in just 55 m^2 of retail space, Sneakerology was in need of a refined merchandising system for its new store in Sydney, Australia. In the Facet Studio-designed space, goods are housed in 200-x-600-mm plywood-and-resin boxes – a gesture that, according to Facet's director, Olivia Shih, 'has little meaning on its own until it's repeated 281 times over'.

The resulting sneaker wall resembles a museum display; each product is neatly ordered and numbered. Touch panels at the store's centre allow visitors to gain further insight into the background of each artefact: in this case, a specific sneaker. 'Although there is obviously no such field of study as "sneaker-ology",' says Shih, 'our design attempts to capture sneakers in a scholarly fashion.'

facetstudio.com.au

Facet Studio's wall of shoes turns the merchandise at Sneakerology into a museum-like display.

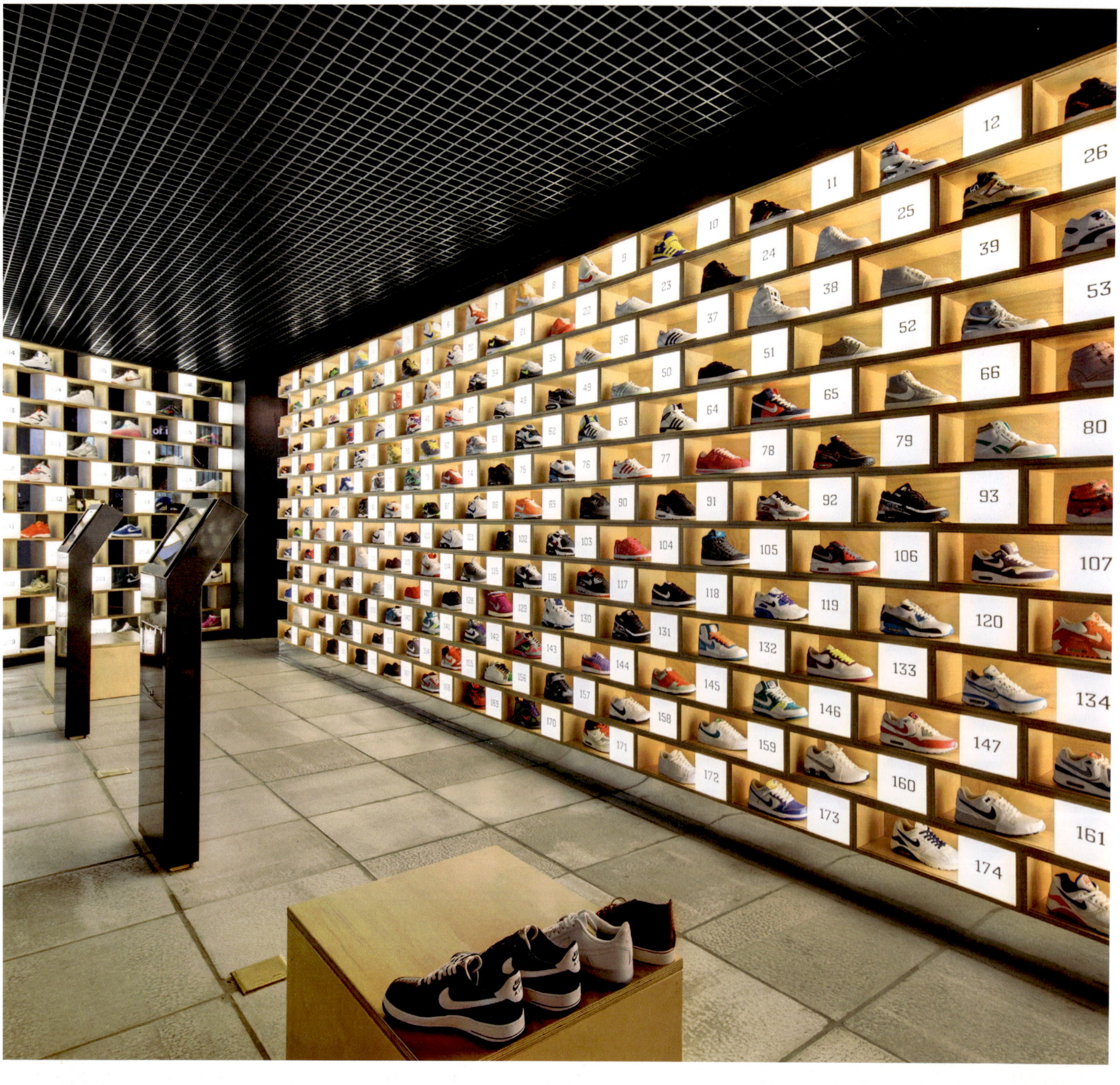

vipp

SOME PEOPLE WILL NEVER BUY IT AGAIN

In 1939, Holger Nielsen designed a waste bin for his wife's hairdressing salon. As she was busy with her hands, the bin needed to be foot-operated. The dentist's wife saw the bin and loved it, since then hundreds of thousands of bins featuring a pedal-operated lid have been manufactured. All with the same simple design and solid construction so you only need to buy a Vipp once. Unless, that is, you want two.

www.vipp.com

Duccio weaves a dream

Words **Onilee Zaborniak**
Photos **Virgile Simon Bertrand**

At Max & Co. in Hong Kong, Duccio Grassi's mysterious volumes lead visitors through a dreamlike odyssey of fashion displays.

Tucked into a shopping mall in the densely developed heart of Hong Kong, Max & Co. is a minimalist's reverie. Aiming for a retail environment that would trigger visions of luxury and tactile excitement, Italian firm Duccio Grassi Architects found inspiration for the new store in daydreaming. Instead of incorporating conventional fashion displays, the designers opted for fluid paths interrupted by areas that 'secretly' reveal the latest trends. These spaces are not meant to withhold wonder, but to act as catalysts in an ongoing dream. 'Clothes are a means to dream,' says Duccio Grassi, 'and retail spaces are a means to clothes.'

Garments displayed on rails inside lacy semicircular enclosures of laser-cut metal promote a sense of spatial movement while rousing shoppers' curiosity. These curved screens appear soft and organic thanks to their juxtaposition with larger, brass elements. 'We followed no predefined rules for the shape and position of the various volumes, which create different areas, both veiled and exposed,' says Grassi. The designer also included touches of oak and polished steel in an interior that takes customers on a serene sartorial journey. Regardless of location, the result is a store from which every shopper surely emerges exclaiming, *Bellissimo*!

ducciograssiarchitects.com

Cleverly
put
together.

DP 01
DECT Phone designed by Jasper Morrison
punktgroup.com

Function. Design. Simplicity.
Punkt.

ARTISAN – NEW FLOORING COLLECTION FUSING HANDICRAFT WITH NEW TECHNOLOGY - WWW.BOLON.COM/ARTISAN

BOLON

Words **Cathelijne Nuijsink**
Photos **courtesy of Yoichi Yamamoto**

Yoichi Yamamoto does it by halves

Last summer in Tokyo, Yoichi Yamamoto surprised pedestrians passing the Issey Miyake boutique in Ginza, the city's famed shopping district, with a display on a platform in the shop window. The scene challenged the viewer's ability to interpret an optical illusion.

The installation featured the backrests of seven wooden chairs, painted blue, randomly positioned across the slightly sloping 'stage'. Completing the picture were chair seats and legs painted in blue on the platform floor. Based on a technique used to create the illusion of depth, the display revealed a small miracle similar to Issey Miyake's 'from 2D cloth to 3D dress' philosophy. 'The best place from which to view the installation was directly in front of the window – right in the middle – at a distance of 2.1 m,' says Yamamoto. 'From there, the three-dimensional puzzle fitted together. Backrests, painted legs and seats blended together optically to become complete chairs.'

Hats designed by Japanese milliner Akio Hirata hung casually from backrests or rested on seats, integrating window display and shop interior, while subtly advertising a retrospective of Hirata's work being held at another Tokyo venue (see *Frame* 82, page 60).

green.dti.ne.jp/yoichi

Yoichi Yamamoto paints 'half chairs' on a flat surface, juxtaposes them with real wooden backrests and produces a sense of such three-dimensionality that your eyes deny what they're seeing.

The perfect prescription from Clavel Arquitectos

'Pharmacy green' gets the ultramodern treatment at Clavel Arquitectos' Farmacia Casanueva.

Words **Suzanne Wales**
Photos **David Frutos Ruiz**

Although globalization has taken its toll on individuality, Spanish high streets still display more character than most. Historically, pharmacies, which play an important role in community life, are representative of architectural trends – hence the large number of Art-Nouveau *farmacias* in northern Spain.

Fast-forward to today, and you'll find a handful of companies working exclusively on the design of ultramodern, functional and eye-catching interiors for chemists. Although that description does not apply to Murcia-based Clavel Arquitectos, the studio recently dipped a toe into the pool of pharmacy design and came up with Farmacia Casanueva.

Taking advantage of prefabricated components, the designers transformed the space within two months, during which time the store continued to operate. The 180-m^2 establishment features a cleanly tiered composition of curving white display units set against a vivid backdrop of metallic slats that cover walls and ceiling in a familiar colour: *farmacia verde*, or 'pharmacy green', is used throughout Spain to identify certain health-related services. An epoxy-resin floor in the same shade completes the picture, creating a fluid interior that wouldn't look out of place in a sci-fi movie. To further clarify the store's purpose, giant letters spelling *farmacia* serve as a solitary window display: a dramatic gesture that doubles as a solar shield.

clavel-arquitectos.com

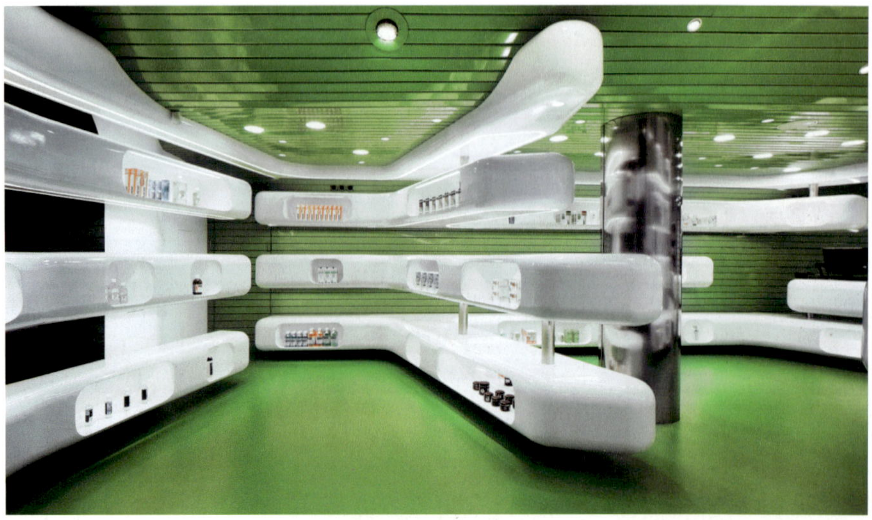

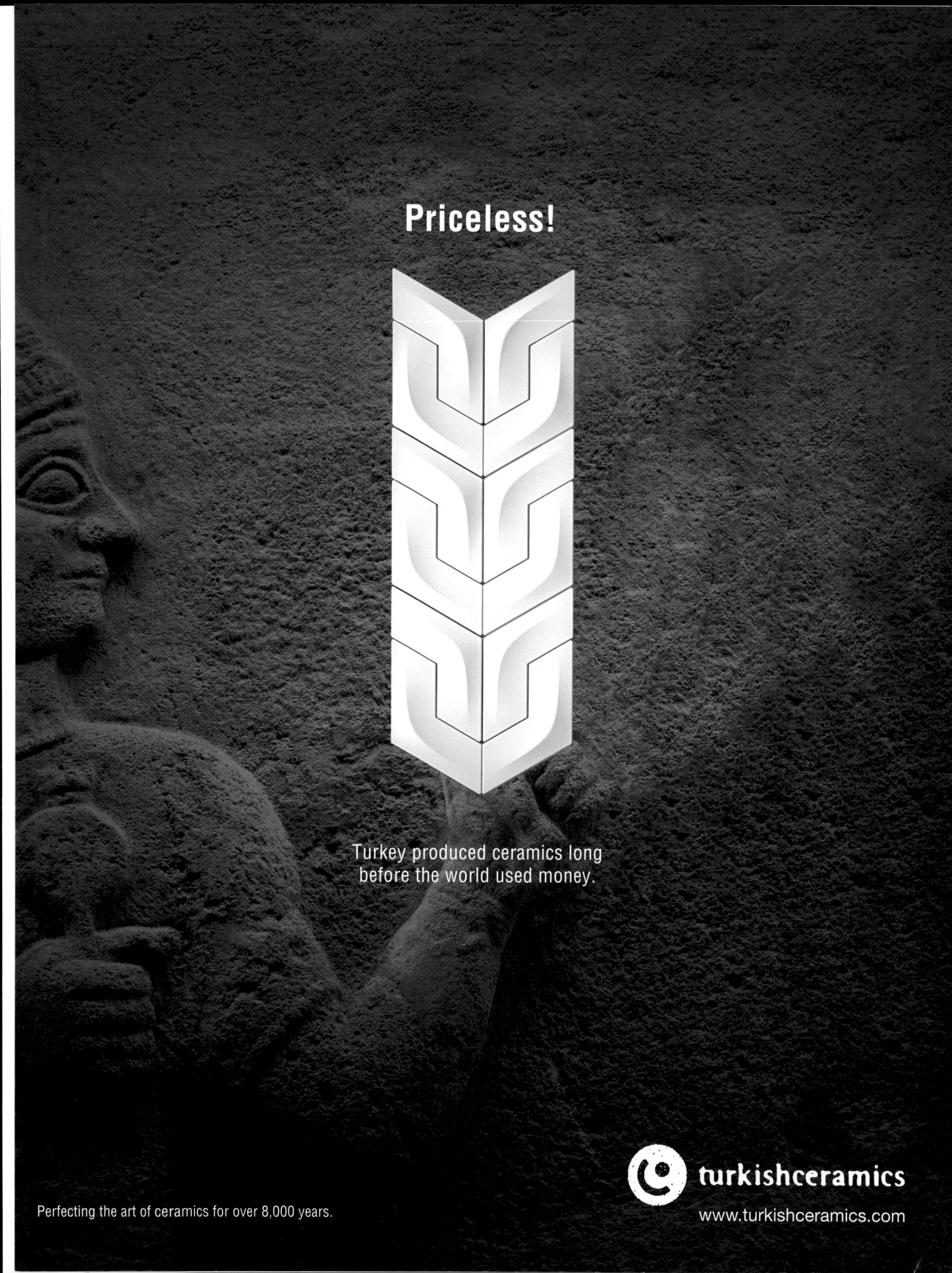
Priceless!
Turkey produced ceramics long
before the world used money.
turkishceramics
Perfecting the art of ceramics for over 8,000 years.
www.turkishceramics.com

JSPR

CAGED BEAUTY

WWW.JSPR.EU

In his first interior-design project, film director David Lynch turns a nightclub into a series of cinematic scenes.

From silver screen to golden scenes

Words **Anna Sansom**
Photos **Alexandre Guirkinger**

Following Arnaud Frisch's request for the design of a Parisian nightclub, David Lynch created the golden setting that is Silencio: the American film director's interior-design debut. 'In Lynch's eyes, gold is simply a beautiful shade of yellow,' says French designer Raphael Navot, who worked with Enia Architects to interpret Lynch's drawings. 'The biggest challenge is how to use gold in a manner that is neither tacky nor flat.'

A patchwork of squares clad in gold leaf and brass meanders across wooden surfaces from the bar to the cavernous art library. 'All the spaces are linked to one another, like scenes in a movie,' says Navot. 'The club features many motifs from Lynch's world and includes yellow, red and blue [on the dance floor].'

Silencio, a reference to the club in Lynch's *Mulholland Drive*, is a luxe-glam addition to after-hours entertainment in the City of Light. According to Navot, Lynch finds elegance 'boring'. 'At Silencio, we have achieved an atmosphere that is both luxurious and warm, in a deeply gentle manner. Curious!'

davidlynch.com

LIMITED EDITION
Living floors
CARPET VISION PINK STAR MATERIAL WOOL-POLYESTER MADE IN BELGIUM
WWW.LE.BE

Double-daring design from Fred Mafra

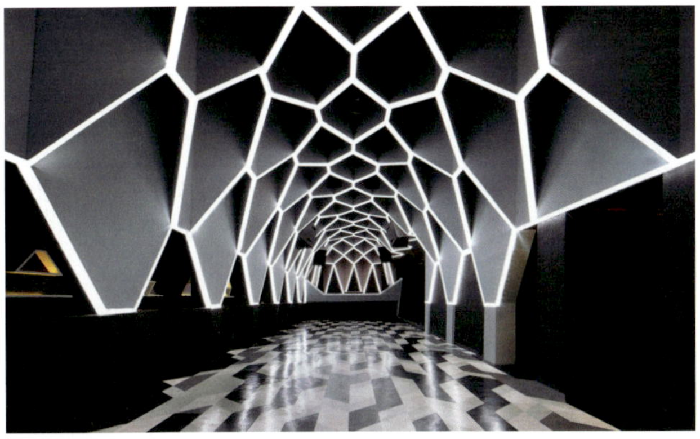

In redesigning his original work, Fred Mafra updated a Brazilian dance club for today's patrons.

Words **Tracey Ingram**
Photos **Jomar Bragança**

Not many designers get a chance to revise their own work, but that's just what happened to Fred Mafra. Four years after designing the Josefine/Roxy club in Belo Horizonte, Brazil, Mafra received an opportunity to update the original. Appreciating the freedom gained from 'previously mastering the space', the designer relished the chance to rework the club for today's patrons. Making use of new technologies, he incorporated colour-changing LED lighting above the narrow, 30-m-long dance floor. A cloud of hexagons – the key shape used throughout the space – forms a prismatic display for revellers below.

Alongside the dance floor, a bar comprising seven bays incorporates an acoustic system that allows bartenders to hear orders clearly. Without a croaky, morning-after voice, visitors are free to spread the word about Brazil's new nightspot. 'Guests seem to be very impressed,' says Mafra. 'The club is always full, and a queue trails down the block.'

fredmafra.com.br

Ellen Sander used cardboard of varying thicknesses for her meeting-room pavilion. She also designed spiralling enclosures and lanterns.

Ellen Sander unplugs a bank

Marking the pavilion designed by Ineke Hans, which accommodates a seafood restaurant, is a pattern in a typically Dutch shade of blue.

Words **Femke de Wild**
Photos **Alexander van Berge**

Emma Architects designed nestlike meeting pavilions made from timber harvested in the Netherlands.

Although the project wasn't completed on schedule, the ground and first floors of Rabobank Netherlands' new headquarters in Utrecht are now open and in use. Linking the two towers that Kraaijvanger Urbis Architects designed and realized – close to a number of existing buildings occupied by the Dutch bank – is a large covered plaza dubbed 'the Square'. Brought in to do the interior design of both towers and plaza, Ellen Sander followed the Rabobank Unplugged philosophy, a concept based on activity-orientated work that shuns the conventions of fixed workstations and a nine-to-five day at the office.

The 'urban plan' that Sander developed for the vast entrance level uniting the towers features zones for waiting, meeting, and having coffee or lunch. Another area has been set aside for the exhibition of pieces from the Rabobank's collection of contemporary art. Because cooperation is such a significant spearhead of Rabo's Unplugged approach to work, Sander invited other designers to contribute to the project. She aimed for a sense of coherence by requesting that everyone involved work with wood. Rather than taking her suggestion literally, Richard Hutten came up with an espresso bar poised beneath a flaring canopy that doubles as a large LED screen for the display of all sorts of images, including trees. Next Architects combined wood and fabric in its design of 'the Bakery'. Emma Architects provided nestlike meeting rooms, and Ineke Hans put her stamp on the seafood restaurant, among other things. Yet another member of the multi-collaboration was Pentagram, but what appeals most to the imagination is the cardboard pavilion designed by Sander herself. As we go to press, the interior design of the towers remains uncompleted; the building will be ready for use between late 2011 and early 2012.

sander.nl

ON THE CUTTING EDGE BETWEEN DESIGN, CRAFTS, FASHION, ART AND ARCHITECTURE

OBJECT ROTTERDAM

LAS PALMAS, LP 11 WILHELMINAKADE 326 3072 AP ROTTERDAM

9-12 FEBRUARY 2012

NEW PARTICIPANTS, NEW PARTNERS, NEW PROGRAM

WWW.OBJECTROTTERDAM.COM

Dominique Coulon's brights on white

Words **Chris Scott**
Photos **Eugeni Pons**

The Josephine Baker School in La Courneuve, just outside Paris, is the latest addition to a new urban development aimed at replacing 1960s housing blocks in the area. Designed by Dominique Coulon et Associés, the 6500-m^2 complex includes a nursery, primary school, leisure centre, classrooms, auditorium, restaurant, office and play areas.

A series of stark, white buildings – which can be reached from a triangular central courtyard surrounded by playgrounds and sports facilities – is offset by accents of bold orange, the various shades of which appear to shift from yellow to red throughout the day, depending on the position of the sun. According to the architects, the colour works well with the blue or grey of the Parisian sky.

The highly graphic result fulfils the architects' desire for a building that is clean, refined, pure and minimal. Despite its architecturally austere presence, the school is warm and welcoming, thanks to a well-considered design that is much appreciated by parents and thoroughly enjoyed by pupils.

coulon-architecte.fr

Orange accents – which appear to shift in colour with the sun's ever-changing light – offset the stark, white façades of the Josephine Baker School.

Prismatic primaries from Mestura

Words **Suzanne Wales**
Photos **Pegenaute**

Schools in Spain – and in most of Europe – are often either centuries-old structures handed down by religious organizations or brand-new designs purpose-built with public funds. New primary schools in Spain must now provide two *patis* (outdoor spaces), one for infants and another for older children. For this reason, most new school designs are U-shaped, with a small, sheltered area in the centre and another on the periphery – a layout that was employed by Mestura in its design of a school in Cornellà de Llobregat, a working-class satellite of Barcelona.

CEIP 2L School (which also has a less complicated name: Martinet) is wedged between a noisy motorway flyover and a football pitch – not exactly the ideal location for kids to spend their formative years. Against the backdrop of red-brick residential blocks, Mestura's three concrete, low-rise volumes seem surprisingly serene. An adjacent skate park serves as a hangout for local youths.

Classrooms occupy the tallest building, whose simple yet ingenious south-facing façade is clad in a fabric of stoneware ceramic tiles. Set at right angles and glazed in various colours, they provide a dazzling visual element while also diffusing the sun's rays.

mestura.es

Mestura's wall of undulating stoneware ceramic tiles is a visual treat for Martinet's primary-school students.

Always want something new, something different? Well, the waiting's over!* Chassis. Wilkhahn.

* A world first in furniture design, the Chassis frame is created by state-of-the-art auto-engineering technologies. Result – an intriguingly lightweight, resilient and exceptionally comfortable chair. So if your interior or lifestyle demands something silky-smooth, visually vibrant or, well, downright eccentric, you've just found it! Interested? For more info visit www.wilkhahn.com

A reading room with 6000 views

Occupying an overwhelming space, the Kanazawa Umimirai Library was designed to stimulate interaction and to offer a physical experience beyond e-books.

Words **Masaaki Takahashi**
Photos **Satoshi Asakawa**

More and more public buildings in Japan are adopting an informal, relaxed atmosphere, and libraries are no exception. Rising from the site of a former factory in Kanazawa, the light, spacious library designed by Kazumi Kudo and Hiroshi Horiba of Coelacanth K&H Architects is seen as a landmark of redevelopment activity in this area.

Horiba compares the building to a box containing a delicious slice of cake. More than simply a place to store books, he says the Umimirai Library was designed to generate 'fun with books' and interaction among users. 'Its structure is like a box that covers an open reading space. Vertical force is carried by small columns, and the impact of a possible earthquake is absorbed by the exterior walls.'

Because heavy snowfall in Kanazawa makes the use of skylights difficult and because direct sunlight damages books, the architects punctured the walls with 6000 circular openings that welcome diffused daylight into the space. Despite the dimensions – a 45-m^2 interior that soars to a height of 12 m – the library is comfortable in all seasons, thanks to floor heating and air-conditioning, as well as to openings for ventilation in the roof.

coelacanth-kandh.co.jp

Subscribe and Save

Mark – Architecture

House in Leiria by Aires Mateus, published in issue #31. Photo Fernando Guerra/FG+SG

Frame – Design

LN-CC store by Gary Card, published in issue #80. Photo Andrew Meredith

Elephant – Art

Picnic by Joyce Ho, published in issue #6.

Subscribe to *Frame*, *Mark* or *Elephant* magazine and get:

- Up to 35% off the cover price
- 10% discount on any additional subscriptions

frameweb.com

Subscription Form

Choose Subscription

Frame

1 year 6 issues		**€95**
1 year student* 6 issues		**€75**
2 year 12 issues		**€180**
2 year student* 12 issues		**€140**

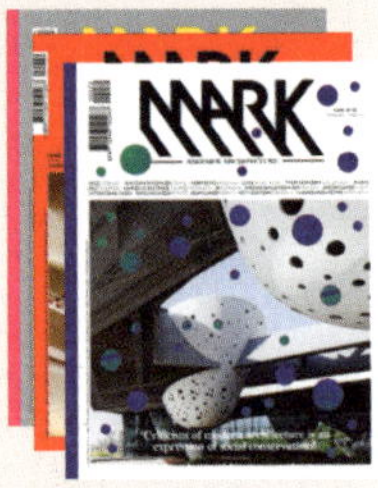

Mark

1 year 6 issues		**€95**
1 year student* 6 issues		**€75**
2 year 12 issues		**€180**
2 year student* 12 issues		**€140**

Elephant

1 year 4 issues		**€65**
1 year student* 4 issues		**€55**
2 year 8 issues		**€120**
2 year student* 8 issues		**€100**

Rates include VAT and shipping costs.
Subscription starts after receipt of payment.

* Students: Please enclose a copy of your student registration form.

10% discount on any additional subscriptions

Return this form via

Email shop@frameweb.com
Fax +31 20 4280 653
Or post to
Frame Publishers
Attn. Subscriptions Department
Laan der Hesperiden 68
1076 DX Amsterdam
The Netherlands

Delivery Address

Name

Company

Address

Post code City

Country

Phone

Email

Payment

Please send me an invoice

Please charge my credit card:

Visa

MasterCard

American Express

Credit card number

Expiry date / (mm/yy)

CVC2 code

(Last 3 digits on the back of your card.
For Amex: 4 digits printed on the front of your card.)

Name of card holder

Signature

HEART MADE.
HAND FINISHED.

LAUFEN bathrooms are created with Swiss precision and high quality demands. Combined with the love for detail, exceptional bathroom concepts come to life: ILBAGNOALESSI One, design by Stefano Giovannoni

LAUFEN

Bathroom Culture since 1892 www.laufen.com

Moroso Spa
Cavalicco, Udine/Italy
T +39 0432 577111
e-mail: info@moroso.it
www.moroso.it
la Biennale di Venezia
54. Esposizione Internazionale d'Arte
Sponsor supporter
MOROSO
Memory armchair
by Tokujin Yoshioka
Moon armchair
by Tokujin Yoshioka
Kub table
by Nendo
Carpet reloaded
for Moroso
photo Alessandro Paderni / ad Designwork

The library encourages interactivity through cantilevered drawers, mobile lab stations and a roving multimedia projector.

NHDM and the art of the library

Words **Tracey Ingram**
Photos **courtesy of Nam June Paik Art Center**

The term 'library' once conjured up images of stacks of books – or the building that housed them. US-based designers Nahyun Hwang and David Eugin Moon (NHDM) are aware that, nowadays, the meaning has changed to include any collection, whether tangible or not. In designing Nam June Paik Library in Yongin, South Korea, the pair aimed to collect, preserve and provide access to the historical and contemporary works of Korean-born American artist Nam June Paik.

'The concept is based on the artist's notion of "random access",' says Moon. 'He proposed a user experience that relies on the controlled access of information but also allows for juxtapositions of unexpected materials throughout the process.'

The library encourages interactivity through cantilevered drawers, mobile lab stations and a roving machine that projects multimedia both inside and outside the space. Projected images become layered on the transparent, polycarbonate panels, 'collapsing the one-dimensionality of typical, institutional libraries', says Moon.

The designers note that the nature of libraries has evolved throughout history, depending on what new technologies or media have been introduced. 'I admire the rigour of these developments,' says Moon. 'When transforming such spaces, however, we need to be prudent in maintaining libraries along with all their spatial and social typologies.'

nhdm.net

Ryo Yamada's forest of light and wind

Photo Ryo Yamada

Words **Cathelijne Nuijsink**

Explaining his latest art installation, Ryo Yamada notes that the term 'landscape' usually 'refers to horizontal scenery. But the word also includes air and sunlight, and that's why I've called my work *Vertical Landscape*.' Exhibited at the Museum of Contemporary Art in Sapporo, Japan, Yamada's installation increased visitors' awareness of wind and sunlight, simple things that many people with busy lives tend to take for granted.

A total of 29 rectangular columns made from translucent synthetic netting of the type used to protect vegetation hung from a roof of netting that spanned the museum's outdoor courtyard. In front of the museum, another 28 columns hanging from panels of netting were also open to the sky. The soft pillars swayed in the breeze while sunlight played on the netting, causing a gentle glisten, a radiant reflection or even a dazzling glare.

'Nowadays, our understanding of nature is mainly scientific. We calculate wind speed in metres per second and temperatures in degrees Celsius,' Yamada says. 'But, like a Buddhist mind, nature never has the same figure or shape. Though this work, I would like people to realize that the environment around us is changing every second.'

ryo-yamada.com

Ryo Yamada's landscape of translucent swaying, light-reflecting columns embodies our continuously changing environment.
Photo Yoshiaki Maezawa

nuuun
kitchens
The Cube Kitchen
design by Maciej Karpiak
nuuun.eu Showroom MEME Design Rijnstraat 165 1079 HD Amsterdam mobile 0031(0) 657319282 info@memedesign.nl

porcupine™
DESALTO
25 table
BF&P 2011
www.desalto.it
johan beentjes
info@johanbeentjes.nl
tel + 31 (0)207 370 911

Artist in residence

Words **Alexandra Onderwater**
Photos **Sergio Pirrone**

Surrounded by trees in Santa Sofia de lo Caña, an area just east of Santiago de Chile, is a dark box constructed from reinforced concrete. The present occupant, an artist, asked architect Juan Augustín Soza to convert an existing house into a dwelling with a creative feel that would also provide privacy and protection. It was a sensitive project, says Soza, particularly because the original design had been honoured at the Quito Pan-American Architecture Biennale. 'We wanted the new house to be autonomous but also to possess the same architectural quality that the prizewinning design had.'

Although the 60-m² volume appears to be sealed off from the outside world, light floods the interior through a glazed section of the roof. Playing the starring role within the brilliance of the white-plastered interior is a centrally positioned, asymmetric patio. Arranged around this courtyard are living, cooking and sleeping areas – but these are not carefully delineated rooms. 'I didn't start designing with a specific image in mind. The solution emerged from my search for a source of daylight and from my efforts to satisfy the client's brief.'

Architect Juan Augustín Soza used a centrally positioned, asymmetric patio to create living, cooking and sleeping areas within an elongated interior.

"THE BEST FRIEND ON EARTH OF MAN IS THE TREE.
WHEN WE USE THE TREE RESPECTFULLY AND ECONOMICALLY,
WE HAVE ONE OF THE GREATEST RESOURCES ON THE EARTH."
- Frank Lloyd Wright
Unmilled Barnwood - Suitable for underfloor heating
ebonyandco
handcrafted solid wood floors
www.ebonyandco.com
Amsterdam Herengracht 516 1017CC +31 (0)20 616 3444 amsterdam@ebonyandco.com
Worldwide Showrooms New York Dublin London Amsterdam Moscow Barcelona

A walk in the park with TNA

Concrete ramps replace stairs in Mist House, and expansive windows blur the boundaries between inside and outside.

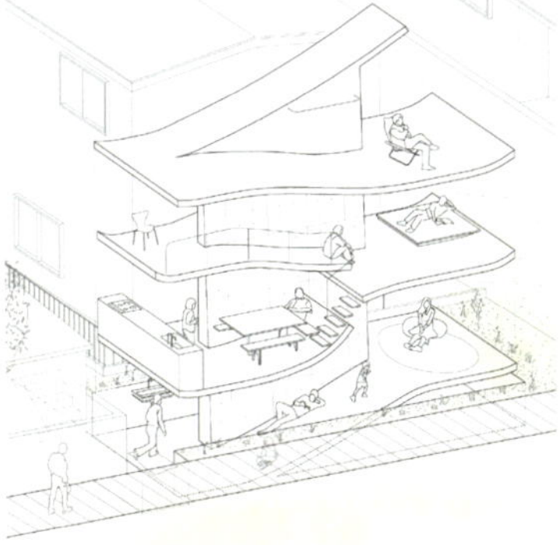

Words **Cathelijne Nuijsink**
Photos **Daici Ano**

In a residential area close to the Tama River in Tokyo, narrow canals separate the various parcels of land. Concrete slabs laid over the canals cover the water completely and function as pavements for pedestrians. Commissioned to design and build a new house in this neighbourhood, architects Makoto Takei and Chie Nabeshima of TNA drew inspiration from the locale's meandering paths and the tiny public spaces on either side of them.

Instead of ordinary flights of stairs, the residents of Mist House ascend from level to level over ramps, as if taking a leisurely outdoor walk along the canal. 'All floors in this house provide places to pause and read a book, take a nap or drink tea,' says Takei, explaining that the floors, which have the same comfortable contours you'd expect to find in a reclining chair or a sofa, represent a new kind of *engawa*, the porch-like extension often found in a traditional Japanese home. 'The difference between an *engawa* and our design,' says Nabeshima, 'is that the former is just a flat wooden surface that projects from the edge of the house, whereas our concrete verandas are integrated into the interior.'

tna-arch.com

Hironaka Ogawa goes out on a limb

Words **Cathelijne Nuijsink**
Photo **Daici Ano**

A contemporary extension to a traditional Japanese house brings the outdoors inside.

'When I first visited the site, all my previous ideas were blown out of the water.' Hironaka Ogawa is talking about the design of a modern addition to a traditional house built 35 years ago in Takamatsu, Japan. Two trees outside the house – a camphor and a zelkova – had such a prominent presence that they were impossible to ignore. Because the site was simply too small for Ogawa to build next to the trees, he had them cut down. Certain branches were removed and others trimmed. Off site, the trees were treated with smoke and dried for two weeks before being returned to their original locations, where they became a feature of the new interior. 'Rather than retaining the existing scenery,' says Ogawa, 'I used it to build new scenery.'

Low-level ribbon fenestration breaks up the walls of the boxlike extension. 'If I had chosen glass walls, the residents would have felt like stuffed specimens in a science museum showcasing two reused yet completely dead trees,' says Ogawa. 'A man and his wife live in the adjoining residence. If they want to see the trees, they have to visit their daughter in the extension.'

ogaa.jp

www.antoniolupi.it_grid, design riccardo fattori_panta rei, tape, design carlo colombo_0X, on_off, design nevio tellatin_servoretto, design mario ferrarini_ayati, design massimo broglio_komodo, design al studio_a.d. riccardo fattori_ph. zerotremedia
MAISON&OBJET_PARIS
20/01/2012_24/01/2012
Pad.8A Stand A13
Showroom
MILANO_ Porta Tenaglia
antoniolupi

gan
www.gan-rugs.com
Materia design Mario Ruiz
Hand Tufted Rug
GANDIA BLASCO
T. +34 902 530 302
Contact in Holland
T. +32 (0) 475 520 220
info@bpropos.com
GAN is a brand of
GANDIA BLASCO

Glasgow's glory meets Zaha Hadid

Words **Grant Gibson**
Photos **Alan McAteer**

Zaha Hadid's Riverside Museum celebrates Glasgow's transport, engineering and shipbuilding legacy with a design that refers to waves on the River Clyde.

Over recent years it seems that Glasgow, best known for the architecture of Alexander 'Greek' Thomson and Charles Rennie Mackintosh, has been collecting buildings from a new generation of influential architects. Foster and Partners completed the Scottish Exhibition and Conference Centre in 1997 (the firm's National Arena Scotland is still under construction), while David Chipperfield was responsible for the BBC Scotland HQ in 2007. Now the name of Zaha Hadid can be added to the list.

The practice's €84.5-million Riverside Museum celebrates the city's transport, engineering and shipbuilding legacy. Glazed at both ends and shaped like a truncated 'S' in plan, the building forms a link between the city and the adjacent River Clyde. The roof-line has apparently been designed to reflect the waves on the water. Inside, the column-free space includes more than 3000 exhibits in over 150 interactive displays, including the re-creation of a city street from the 1900s, vintage cars, steam locomotives, trams, motorbikes and even skateboards.

According to Hadid, the museum represents 'a true demonstration and celebration of the skills and passion of local engineers and contractors who helped bring this building to life'.

zaha-hadid.com

CALL FOR ★ ENTRIES

★ FRAME moooi AWARD ★ 2012

THE JURY ★ PHILIPPE STARCK ★

WHAT
★ Furniture and lamps custom-designed for a specific interior

WHO
★ Interior designers, product designers and architects

WHEN
★ Submit your work between 1 September and 1 December, 2011

HOW
★ Upload your entry to framemoooi.com

PRIZE
★ €25,000

The award ceremony will be during *Salone del Mobile* 2012 in Milan.

framemoooi.com

Vibrantly coloured partitions and ceilings in a predominantly matte-black interior lead the way at the Balenciaga Museum in Getaria, Spain.

Colour fields make fashion history

Words **Alexandra Onderwater**
Photos **Iñigo Bujedo Aguirre**

Asked to turn a ginormous box of blocks into an intimate yet eloquent fashion museum, what do you do? When his firm was commissioned to do the interior design of the Balenciaga Museum in Getaria, a village in Spain's Basque region, architect Toño Foraster of AV62arquitectos remarked that 'trying to make this building elegant would be stupid'.

'The building has extraordinary proportions and was designed by the mayor's very dear friend, a Cuban architect – but that's another story,' says Foraster. 'The authorities organized a competition for the design of the interior, which we won. After a great deal of discussion, we used matte-black surfaces throughout in an attempt to reduce the impact of the dimensions.'

Fields of bright colour function as a signage system, with orientation points that indicate where visitors can find the restaurant, the stairs, the cloakroom and other facilities. 'We certainly didn't want to interpret or duplicate Balenciaga's work,' says Foraster. 'We treated his designs as art, grouping the dresses into six categories and displaying them in glass cases on the first and second floors. Our design includes nothing that detracts from his creations.'

av62arquitectos.com

© TERZANI 2011
STREAM,
IRIDESCENT
LIGHT.
TERZANI
LA LUCE PENSATA
TERZANI (ITALY) - INFO@TERZANI.COM - WWW.TERZANI.COM

Into the blue with Toyo Ito

Words **Cathelijne Nuijsink**
Photos **Daici Ano**

Looking for a good mix of architecture, art and nature? A great place to start is an archipelago in Japan's Seto Inland Sea, where avant-garde art and the museums in which it is displayed – buildings designed by some of the country's top architects, including Ryue Nishizawa, Kazuyo Sejima and Hiroshi Sambuichi – blend beautifully into the topography of the islands. Recently added to the list of existing *tours de force*, but on the other side of the sea, is the Toyo Ito Museum of Architecture, which Ito himself realized on picturesque Omishima Island.

Architecture aficionados, in particular, will appreciate the design of the museum's two buildings. Like much of the work in Ito's *oeuvre*, Steel Hut, which he calls 'a pavilion for exhibitions', explores extraordinary structural forms and their potential. The five exhibition spaces are composed of four distinctive polyhedrons, which give each room slanted walls. Visitors touring the interior become privy to every detail of the architect's career. A replica of Silver Hut, the name given to Toyo Ito's Tokyo residence (1984), was also erected on the museum site.

toyo-ito.co.jp

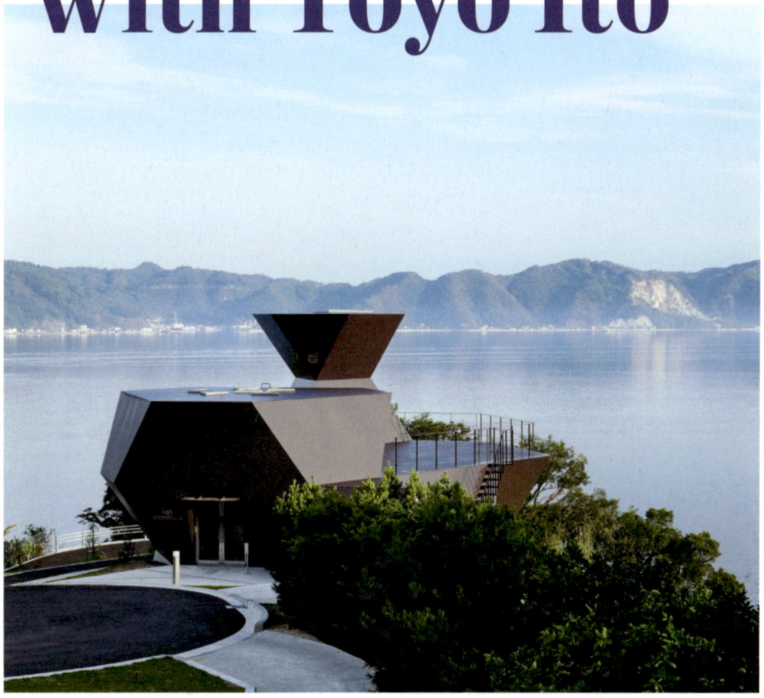

Steel Hut, one of the Toyo Ito Museum of Architecture's two buildings, is composed of four distinctive polyhedrons that form five exhibition spaces.

Souto de Moura's obsessive oeuvre

Words **Carlos M Guimarães**
Photos **José Campos**

Concursos 1979-2010, a travelling exhibition devoted to 2011 Pritzker Prize winner Eduardo Souto de Moura, is a tribute to the architect's specific approach to design and to the methods he uses. It debuted at Oporto's Architecture School (FAUP), where it was the first presentation to honour the work of the former student and professor. Portuguese design agency R2, an outfit with a strong background in graphic design, created the entire exhibition space.

Instead of focusing on built projects, along with glossy photographs of the results, the show's organizers, André Campos and Pedro Guedes de Oliveira, wanted to reveal the intense and sometimes obsessive process behind Souto de Moura's *oeuvre*. On display in the two-room exhibition gallery of the Álvaro Siza-designed school in Oporto were sketches, detail drawings, physical models, photomontages, photographs and historical data relating to 50 projects prepared for competitions between 1979 and 2010.

High walls covered in drawings demonstrate what the exhibition catalogue has to say. The show celebrates 'an informed architecture, produced with conceptual accuracy, commitment, engagement . . . like a scientist who searches for a solution and an artist who knows precisely the path he does not want to take'.

r2design.pt

In R2's design of an exhibition featuring the work of Eduardo Souto de Moura, sketches explain a great deal about the architect's approach to creating buildings.

One concept, more than 8,000 chairs: With the ID Chair Concept, everyone will find the office swivel chair that is right for them. All of the chairs are ergonomic. A study carried out at the Swiss Federal Institute of Technology Zurich supports this claim. Companies benefit from the aesthetics, which bring about a unified visual appearance, and from the Green User Agreement, a comprehensive service offer that ensures long-term use of the ID Chair Concept.

More information: www.vitra.com/ID

vitra.

Remodelling the Market

Combining the nostalgia of local trading with the convenience of superstores, a new breed of market is in town.

Moscow's Tsvetnoy Central Market is dominated by a 2000-m^2 ceiling made from beaten stainless steel that reflects the movement and colours of the food stalls below.
Photo Chris Gascoigne

Words **Giovanna Dunmall**

If you take an escalator to the top of Tsvetnoy Central Market, a luxury department store in central Moscow, you are greeted by a buzzing food hall filled with fresh produce, hot-food counters, cafés, bars, restaurants and three outdoor terraces with breathtaking views. The overall space, which includes a mezzanine, is dominated by a striking 2000-m^2 ceiling made from beaten stainless steel. The vast overhead surface reflects the movement and colours of the food market through two full-height atria.

'The idea of a strong visual connection from the lower floors to the food hall played a big part in the development of the concept,' says project director Chris Waite of London-based architecture practice Lifschutz Davidson Sandilands. The feature ceiling has 2600 individual panels with customized shapes and embossed patterns. Capturing the reflection of shoppers moving below, the surface is a constantly changing element. 'The effect is dazzling,' he says with evident pride.

Working closely with food consultants Ford McDonald, Lifschutz Davidson Sandilands was keen to bring back the colourful atmosphere and spirit of 19th-century Moscow, when flower stalls lined the street and the city's Central Market, popular during the Soviet era, stood on the site of the current department store. 'At its height, the market was packed with produce from right across the union, as well as goods imported from central Asia. It had a souk-like appeal,' says Waite.

While many recent food-retail projects evoke images of traditional markets, there's also been a focus on offering the breadth and convenience of goods we find in supermarkets, as well as opportunities to eat and hang out with friends. A good example is US organic grocery chain Whole Foods Market – which also has outlets in the UK and Canada – and its canny mix of wooden carts piled high with fresh produce alongside shelves of specialist gourmet food.

In Madrid's trendy Chueca neighbourhood, one of the city's older

A converted greenhouse is home to Landmarkt, which offers shoppers locally farmed food in a rustic setting in North Amsterdam.
Photo Thijs Uylenbroek

markets – the Mercado San Antón – reopened in May with a sleek, new look and *Nuevo* added to its name. The brick-and-glass structure appears somewhat ungainly from the residential street outside, but the interior's massive, light-filled atrium lends the space an airy, contemporary feel. Visitors to the renovated market can shop for fresh produce, meat and fish at ground level and, on the mezzanine, enjoy tapas, sushi and smoothies at one of the establishment's eateries. Topping the complex is La Cocina de San Antón, a restaurant whose patrons – after opting for a market view or a spot on the terrace – can have chefs prepare the fresh products they just bought below. Traditionalists of all ages have voiced their disappointment with the inevitably higher prices and the loss of yet another authentic Madrid market, but many of the younger locals have responded with enthusiasm.

Markus Konings – manager of the design team for Landmarkt, a new indoor farmers' market just north of Amsterdam – has a pragmatic take on the transformation of the traditional market. 'We believe the original market will survive, but it has to adjust,' he says. 'People have less time these days and prefer to get all their groceries in one place. They are looking for tasty, healthy food with known origins, which is not possible in traditional markets. Concepts like Whole Foods, Stew Leonard's and Landmarkt can fulfil such needs.'

As its name suggests, the food at Landmarkt is produced by area farmers. And the setting, a converted greenhouse, is appropriately 'rough and natural'. Dotting the concrete floor is an assortment of wooden pallets, wheeled carts, baskets and crates – all displaying fresh produce. To get the 'unfinished' feeling he wanted, Konings asked for a bit of 'intentional deviation in the details'. Diners sitting at rustic wooden tables in Landmarkt's plant-filled restaurant savour regional dishes made with ingredients fresh from the market.

These days, it seems we seek the solace and reassurance of a traditional market with lots of extra bells and whistles. Rest assured, the reinvention of food retail is set to continue.

lifschutzdavidson.com
kkaa.co.jp
landmarkt.nl

We seek the reassurance of a traditional market with extra bells and whistles

Kengo Kuma combines a hotel and market in Yusuhara, Japan.
Photo courtesy of Kengo Kuma

New fashion, old passion...
cebi®
DECORATIVE
FURNITURE
FITTINGS
cebidesign.com
Tel: (+90216) 430 81 81 Fax: (+90216) 430 81 85 cebi@cebidesign.c

Reggiani Re Lighting. Retail is detail.

The Reggiani project for retail is to highlight any details of the product and of the shopping space. Attention to detail can make the difference between average and outstanding. Reggiani Illuminazione Inc. offers hundreds of design combinations, accurate tailor-made solutions with excellent quality of light and extraordinary efficiency. Reggiani means technological expertise, experience and reliability and service on an international scale, in full compliance with the laws and regulations of each single country.

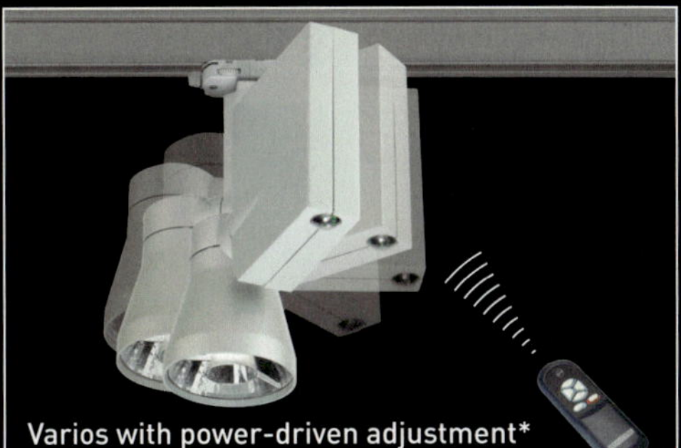

Varios with power-driven adjustment*
Design: L.A.P.D.

*Technology under licence of Remote Controlled Lighting Ltd

Download Reggiani Re Lighting on App Store or visit: www.relighting-reggiani.net

REGGIANI SPA ILLUMINAZIONE • contact@reggiani.net • www.reggiani.net

REGGIANI
LIGHTING RE-SOLUTIONS

EuroDisplay®
www.eurodisplay.de

'OLO DESIGN ANDREAS STÖRIKO

WWW.LAMMHULTS.COM

Photo Jun Nakamichi (Nacása & Partners)

108
Angle Poise
Wonderwall

Photo Hélène Hilaire

Photo Choo

Features

A Modern

Following the Fukushima earthquake, Teruhiro Yanagihara moved his studio from Osaka to a typical Japanese residence within the green periphery of Kyoto.

raditionalist

With his new label, Teruhiro Yanagihara is furthering his fusion of contemporary design and Japanese crafts.

Words **Cathelijne Nuijsink**
Photos **Takumi Ota**

The centrepiece of the Ne hair salon in Osaka is a large staircase that serves as a waiting area.

Ne
Interior Design Osaka 2010

Because Yanagihara sees every human being – in this case, every customer and every hair stylist – as unique, he designed the Ne hair salon as a sequence of objects and volumes with distinctive characters. Inside the striking stairway at the centre of the 73-m^2 salon are a rest room and storage space. The multifunctional stairs have been designed to serve as both waiting room and display unit. Mirrors are positioned to resemble pieces of sculpture. Cabinet doors seem to be cut from a blank wall consisting of a single sheet of paper.

'Ne is like a stage for getting the most sophisticated haircut'

Mirrors in the salon resemble pieces of sculpture.

Clean lines and an air of minimalism dominate the interior. In his design for Ne, Yanagihara rejected the idea of a cosy, domestic atmosphere.

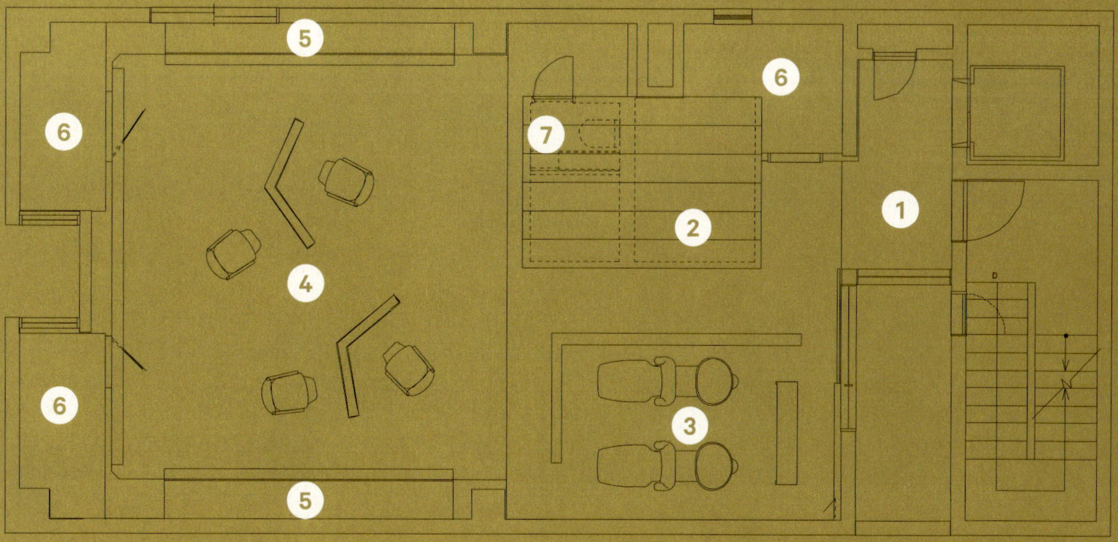

1. Entrance
2. Waiting area
3. Shampoo area
4. Cutting area
5. Light boxes
6. Storage
7. Rest room

Made from two metallic discs, Yanagihara's Chords pendant lamp assumes a different guise from every viewpoint, while creating a varied play of light and shadow.
Photo courtesy of Teruhiro Yanagihara

Yanagihara designed a collection of disposable tableware for *Wallpaper* magazine that the user can assemble from sheets of specially treated paper. The spoon splits to form chopsticks.

For Karimoku New Standard, Yanagihara – who is also the Japanese furniture brand's art director – designed the Nook coat rack, a series of stools, the Halfway sofa and the Pile shelving unit (1-4).
His designs for online gift shop Ringbell include the Tray Table series, a small sofa, a mirror and a fruit bowl (5-9).

1

2

3

4

5

6

7

8

9

After being introduced at the Salone del Mobile, the Karimoku New Standard X Shin Suzuki exhibition was shown at Lidewij Edelkoort's Paris office, where it occupied a larger space than it had in Milan.
Photos Shin Suzuki

Having received furniture from Karimoku New Standard for use in his work, photographer Shin Suzuki shoots hundreds of photos daily, many of which show pieces from the furniture collection in a natural setting.

Karimoku New Standard
Exhibition Design Paris and Milan 2011

In 2009, 70-year-old Japanese brand Karimoku invited Teruhiro Yanagihara to become art director of the company's Karimoku New Standard furniture collection. An exhibition held last summer at Lidewij Edelkoort's Paris office was Karimoku New Standard X Shin Suzuki. Designed and curated by Teruhiro Yanagihara, the show had debuted earlier in the year at the Salone del Mobile. Every day, photographer Shin Suzuki shoots hundreds of photos of himself and his surroundings and posts them on his website: suzukishin.jp. In anticipation of the Milan exhibition, Karimoku New Standard offered Suzuki the use of furniture from its collection, which was then featured in his images in a natural way. During the project, Fukushima, where the Suzuki family lives, was hit by a tsunami. Photos made at that time were also included in the exhibition.

The model for the iceberg structure.

Maquette showing the salon layout.

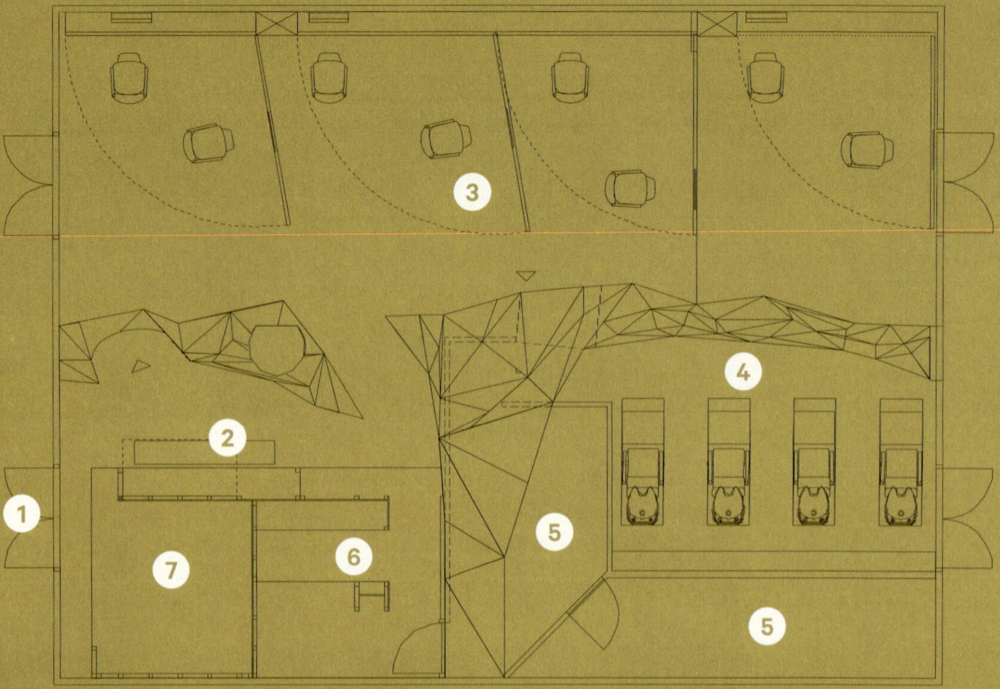

1. Entrance
2. Waiting area
3. Cutting area / event space
4. Shampoo area
5. Storage
6. Reception
7. Gallery

‘The appearance might be minimalist, but the concept is often complex’

Pivoted doors open from the walls to separate the salon into a reception area and spaces for washing and cutting hair.

With a sculptural wall reminiscent of the contours of an iceberg, Yanagihara created an extreme contrast between the historic Raffles Hotel and the beauty salon.
Photos Choo

Kizuki + Lim
Interior Design Singapore 2010

Taking centre stage in Yanagihara's Kizuki + Lim beauty salon are the imposing contours of an iceberg in light grey and fluorescent yellow. The sculptural intervention is in sharp contrast to the salon's location – the historic five-star Raffles Hotel in Singapore. Pivoted doors with mirrors open from the walls of the structure to separate the salon into a reception area and spaces for washing and cutting hair. After hours, these doors can be closed to create a continuous space large enough for small concerts and other events.

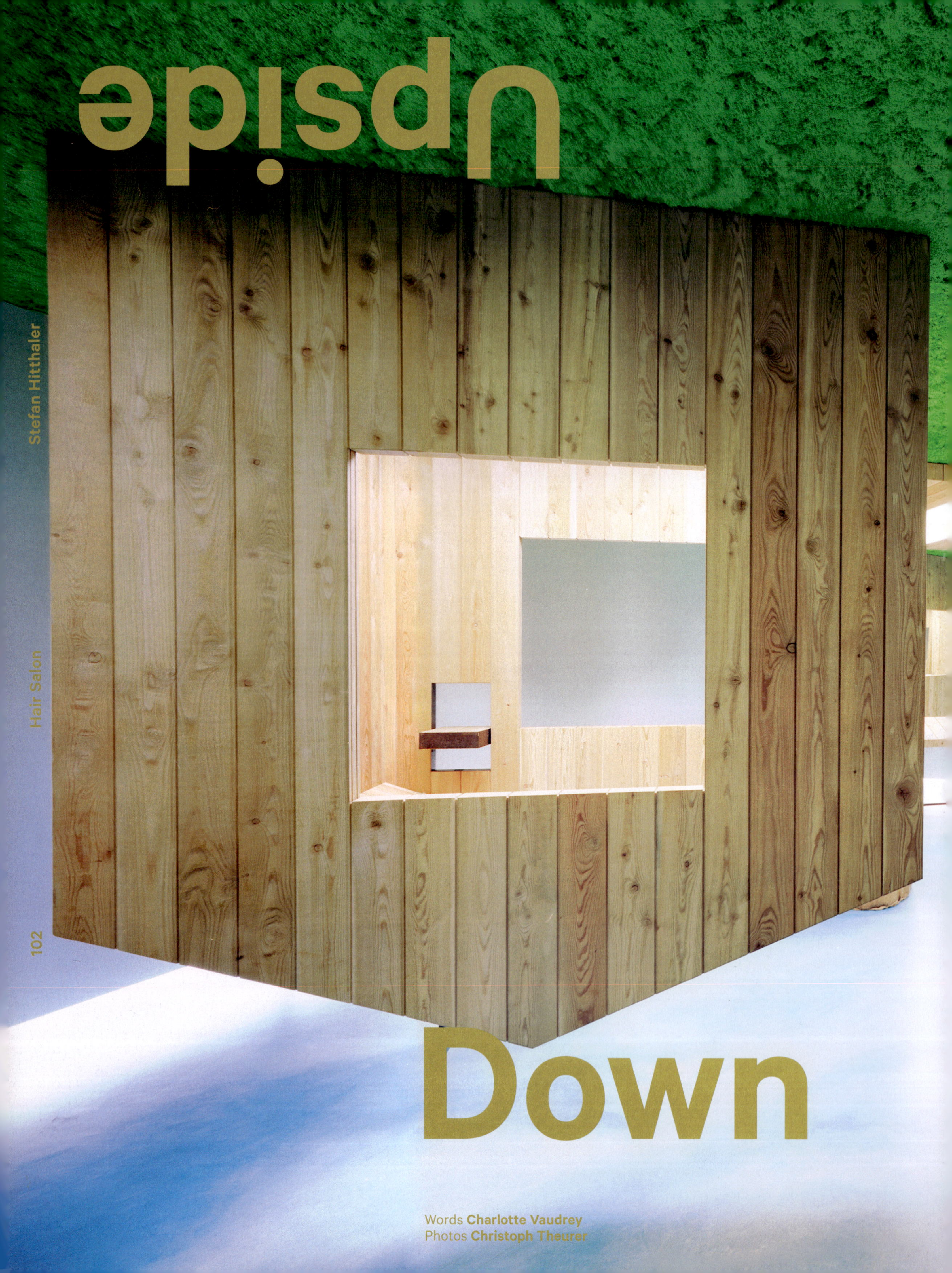

Upside Down

Words **Charlotte Vaudrey**
Photos **Christoph Theurer**

You're Turning Me

A hair salon in rural Italy flips every expectation on its head.

Initially, Hitthaler envisaged locally handcrafted salon chairs, but the required functions were too complex, necessitating the purchase of seats from a manufacturer of salon furnishings.

Conservative locals feared visitors wouldn't accept contemporary interiors

A bar in Monguelfo, a provincial town in northern Italy, is abuzz. The owner of a soon-to-be-opened hair salon, on her way to order a drink, is being accosted from every direction.

'. . . Garden sheds . . .'

'. . . clouds on the ceiling . . .'

'. . . farmhouse furniture next to sleek, black chairs . . .'

'. . . a hair salon? How can it be a hair salon?'

Over the cacophony, the woman appeals to the barista. 'We pulled the paper off the windows only yesterday,' she says. 'How can so many people have seen the salon already?' The barista shrugs. 'Small town?' he mouths, before raising his voice to be heard over the crowd. 'One thing's for sure – everyone's talking about it.' The woman smiles at the expectant faces and the questions still being fired at her. 'You think the ground floor warrants all this attention?' she laughs. 'Just wait until you've seen the basement!'

The location in question is Salon Himmelblau (German for 'sky blue'), the work of local architect Stefan Hitthaler.

The desire to whip up curiosity among passers-by prompted Hitthaler to save the most extraordinary part of the concept for the basement. He relishes the idea that 'diverse worlds exist within the same salon' and that patrons having their hair cut on different floors will compare experiences and generate discussion.

On the ground floor, two fully glazed walls leave no doubt about what has left the people of the small mountain town agog. Arching in a smart apex over each salon chair is an open wooden shelter comprising two walls and a roof. A softly textured, cloudlike ceiling of sprayed concrete looms overhead. Far from representing a garden-shed aesthetic, the insertions are a playful interpretation of the local *maso*, an iconic farmhouse-style building that is reminiscent of the Alpine huts immortalized in *Heidi*. (The tale may have been set across the border, but Heidi's mountain range runs into the ski resort above Monguelfo.) The same level features a floor-to-ceiling lighting installation that looks like a giant E. It hides a structural column, while also providing masterfully subtle signage when lit from behind at night. Strolling by the shop, you can't fail to miss the glowing 'comb' whose teeth form shelving for hair products and magazines.

The concept takes an eye-popping leap further in the basement, where the stylized houses are inverted. With their floors attached to the ceiling of the salon, each mini-***maso*** appears to float, rather poetically, a metre from the ground. Large windows cut into the side panels of each 'house' provide framed views through the space, adding to its dreamlike feel. The sprayed-concrete ceiling, textured to a much greater depth than its ground-level counterpart, is as green as grass, whereas a vibrant skyscape stretches across the resin floor. Customers can literally walk across the clouds to their seats.

Compared with the rather conservatively built projects in Hitthaler's portfolio, the salon stands out as unexpectedly quirky. When I ask what inspired the witty interior, the designer tells me to prepare for a complicated explanation. Born and raised locally, Hitthaler – like 70 per cent of the population in the immediate area – is German, not Italian. His grandfather, also born locally, not only spoke German but ...

The resin floor is a vibrant skyscape. Customers can literally walk across the clouds to their seats.

Existing stairs are clad in raw steel. Working with a local artisan, Hitthaler welded 4-mm-thick cable between the two flights to give them a stitched-together look.

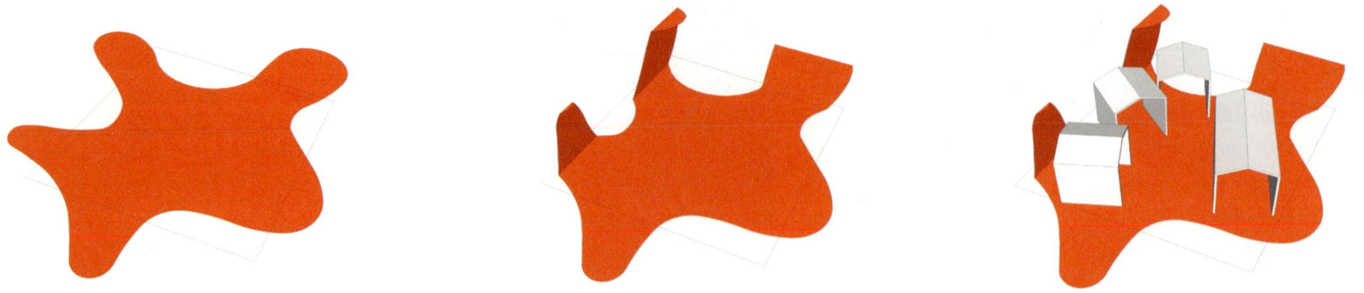

An enormous 'splash of orange paint' – chosen to reflect the owner's personality – moves up the walls and onto the ceiling of the ground floor.

'The tourism industry is keen to sell the rustic image of this once-rural region'

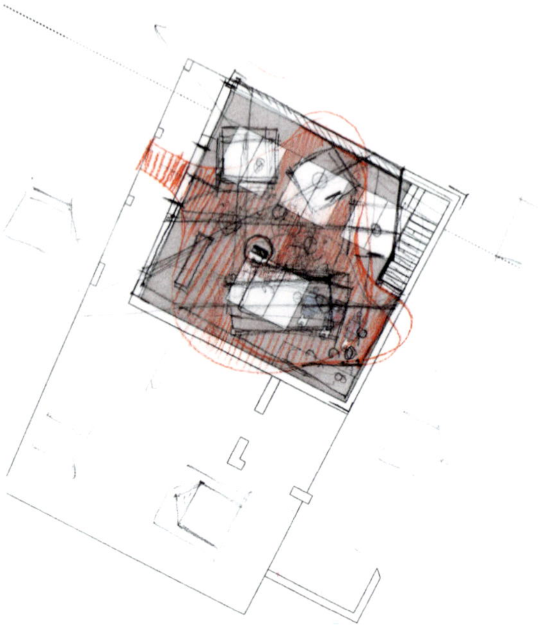

Sketch of the ground floor.

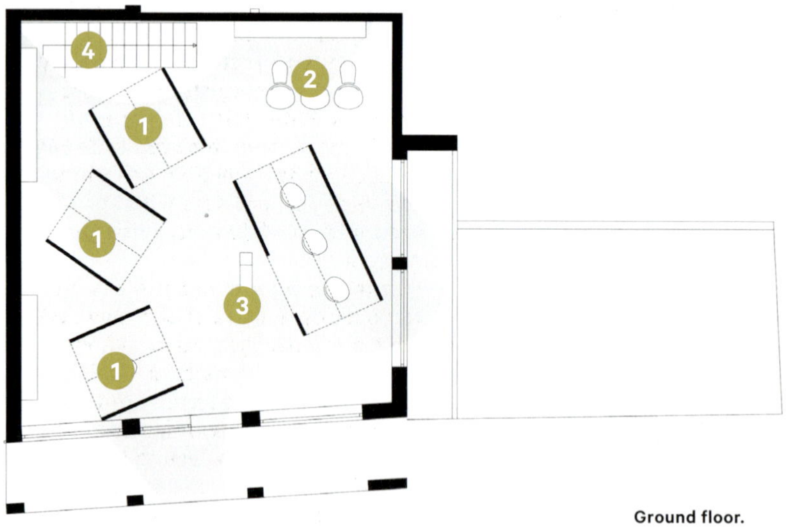

Ground floor.

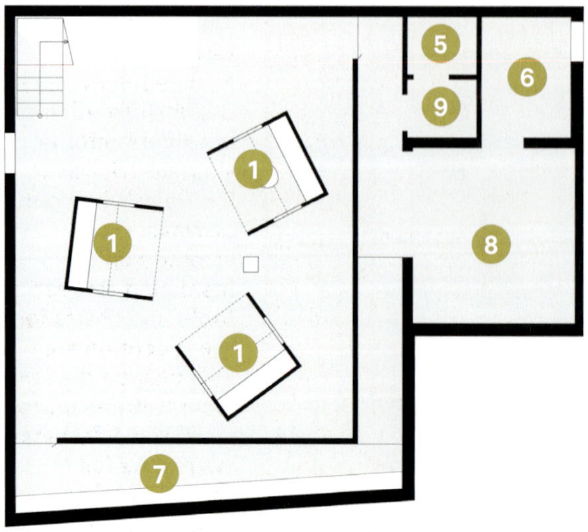

Basement.

1. Hairdressing station
2. Washbasin
3. Shelving display
4. Stairs
5. Rest room
6. Changing room / shower
7. Storage
8. Solarium
9. Stock room

Salon Himmelblau

Location Via Paul Troger 1A, 39035 Monguelfo, Italy
Design Stefan Hitthaler (www.raum.it)
Client Salon Himmelblau
Materials Wood, steel, plaster, resin
Furniture and lighting Custom-made (excluding salon chairs)
Flooring IPM Italia (ipm-italy.it)
Walls Dantone
Area 183 m²
Budget €140,000 - €170,000
Completed December 2010

A floor-to-ceiling lighting installation resembles a giant comb, the teeth of which form shelving for hair products and magazines.

... considered himself Austrian; the region was not part of Italy until after World War I. 'We're a culture between cultures,' says Hitthaler. 'Tremendous tension still exists between Austrian traditions and Italian culture. The older people hold German values dear, while the younger generation finds the Italian way of life more appealing.'

Architecturally speaking, the area is disappointing – thanks in part to Monguelfo's status as a popular holiday destination. 'People who work in the tourism industry are keen to continue selling the rustic image of this once-rural region,' says Hitthaler. There has been a real struggle to create a dialogue between up-and-coming architects who have been educated abroad (Hitthaler studied architecture in Innsbruck, barely 100 km from Monguelfo) and those who want to keep rolling out the mock (read: fake), quaint buildings of yesteryear, as if they are afraid that anything else will scare away tourists. When Hitthaler, now 45, returned home to open his studio 20 years ago, he became enmeshed in an internal struggle to design projects with an international feel while preserving the local Tyrolean culture.

Hitthaler's figurative conflict waged for two decades until he began playing with the traditional Tyrolean building element for Salon Himmelblau. 'As I worked,' he says, 'the internal fight disappeared, leaving me with a sense of freedom. I now have the feeling that these two very different cultures can provide me with incredible influences rather than destroying me.' Finally 'at peace', he produced Himmelblau's delightfully ethereal basement interior. Upstairs, however, Hitthaler's humour prevails. He selected an old-fashioned wooden table and chairs for the reception area as a play on the two local cultures and a wink at old Tyrolean values. As for conservative locals who feared visitors wouldn't accept contemporary architecture or interiors, the success of the salon has proved otherwise.

The owner consolidated two salons, each with three seats, to create the new Himmelblau, adding two stations to make it an eight-seat salon. Not just big by Italian standards, the place is huge for a town whose population barely tips the 6000 mark. Himmelblau attracts both locals and tourists, however – to such an extent that the owner has asked Hitthaler to incorporate another two hairdressing stations into the space. Let's hope the local naysayers are listening. _

Primary shapes are made from local larch, a wood used in the Tyrolean houses that inspired the concept. Here Hitthaler's design displays stylized interpretations of the traditional *maso*.

Raising the Bar

With Ozone, currently the world's highest nightspot, Wonderwall takes cashed-up, cosmopolitan clients to new heights of luxury.

Words **Yoko Choy**
Photos **Jun Nakamichi (Nacása & Partners)**

Guests make a dramatic entrance (and departure) via the black-and-white marble hallway with its mirrored ceiling and softly lit draped curtains.

The entrance hallway (left) opens out on Wonderwall's 'Edenic Experiment': a fantasy evocation of an idealized natural landscape, in which curvy columns are like tree trunks supporting an ornately branching ceiling.

A private dining room combines intimacy and opulence, thanks to a curving wall of marble and gently glowing lighting.

Ritz-Carlton was determined to reach the pinnacle of luxury

Fashionably perched on the 118th floor of the International Commerce Centre (ICC) in Hong Kong, a whopping 490 m from the ground, Ozone claims the crown as the highest bar in the world. Encompassing the top floor of the recently opened Ritz-Carlton Hotel, which occupies the ICC from the 102nd floor up, the 755-m² venue is the place to go for cocktails, contemporary Japanese cuisine, Asian tapas and an amazing panorama of Hong Kong. The exceptional location alone is more than enough to make an impression, but Ritz-Carlton had an even loftier ambition: a new identity. The man invited to come up with an entirely fresh image for the brand's most significant destination in Asia was Japanese architect Masamichi Katayama (46), founder of interior-design firm Wonderwall.

Established in 2000, Wonderwall is best known for its innovative approach to retail environments. A distinctive and potent force in the industry, the firm has a portfolio of noteworthy projects highlighted by showroom spaces for Uniqlo in the USA and Europe, Colette in Paris, Nike in Tokyo, and the Bathing Ape stores in Asia. The team is currently working on a private studio for graffiti artist KAWS in the New York City borough of Brooklyn.

Katayama is not a conventional choice for a traditionalist hotel group like Ritz-Carlton. Having closed its Renaissance-style property three years ago, however, the hotel was out to become a forerunner in contemporary lifestyle and excellence. In choosing Wonderwall to design Ozone, the brand literally crossed the line from conservative to cool, demonstrating its determination to reach the very pinnacle of modern luxury.

Guests enter the hotel lift on the 8th floor of the ICC and, moving at a speed of 9 m per second, arrive precisely 55 seconds later on the 102nd floor, where they step into the Ritz-Carlton's ...

The bar exemplifies the intricate geometric patterning used throughout the design, which was based on Voronoi diagrams. Wooden shelving behind the bar reflects the segmented layered Corian ceiling and marble floor.

Luxurious materials were used in inventive ways. The sushi bar features a backdrop of illuminated yellow onyx panels, fronted and flanked by timber features.

... spacious reception lounge. Awaiting them in one corner are two narrow lifts clad in black leather and mirrors, poised to carry them the remaining 16 storeys to Ozone. When the doors open to reveal the dimly neon-lit foyer on the 118th floor, guests are greeted instantly by sleekly dressed staff. Lining both sides of the space are floor-to-ceiling curtains that contrast with the thunderous, geometrically patterned marble floor and fragmented-glass motif of the ceiling.

Katayama has imbued Ozone with a sense of movement that is evident in both layout and design features. The space includes a sushi bar, an Asian kitchen, and a main bar and lounge area. The signature geometric pattern featured in the foyer continues throughout the interior. It is repeated on walls and ceilings and in different materials to produce interesting layers of texture. Behind the main bar, the pattern is translated into an ivory-toned wooden shelf for wines and spirits. This shelving unit extends to the ceiling, where the pattern becomes part of the lighting scheme. Wraparound bar, stools and couches shine in the dark like irregularly shaped diamonds, and giant spiralling sculptures double as structural columns. The result is a seamless landscape of visual elements forming an imaginary world.

Lighting plays a key role in all of Katayama's designs. Not only does he combine natural and artificial lighting wherever possible; he also uses mirrors and other reflective materials to capture the movements of people, to enlarge a space and to exert a strong influence on the desired ambience. In Ozone's sumptuous dining room, a dazzling plethora of spherical pendants hang from the ceiling, while lighting in the lounge area bathes guests in subtly changing colours. Illumination throughout the various areas enhances the glamorous crowd and extends the beauty of the city below.

Mirrors and reflective surfaces create movement, space and drama

No city in the world has more skyscrapers than Hong Kong. A rooftop club or top-of-the-town bar is hardly a new concept here. Many of the more popular sky-high lounges are on the island itself, but it is the view from Kowloon Peninsula to the city centre across the water that has cemented Hong Kong's reputation as the Pearl of the Orient. The views from Ozone's glass-walled terrace are dramatic – where can you find a more awe-inspiring panorama of the city, the stunning island skyline, Victoria Harbour and the Kowloon Peninsula waterfront? Corner couches offer a 270-degree, million-dollar spectacle. From this height, the island looks like a toy floating on the water.

Even the global economic crisis has not tarnished Hong Kong's position as an international financial heavyweight. The city continues to contribute to the world economy and to attract visitors looking for the best in leisure and entertainment. 'It's an exciting city, where people come for metropolitan experiences,' says Mark DeCocinis, regional vice president and general manager of the Ritz-Carlton Hong Kong. Ozone is a stunning response to the brand's bold intention: to take a young, sexy and cashed-up generation to new heights of luxury. _

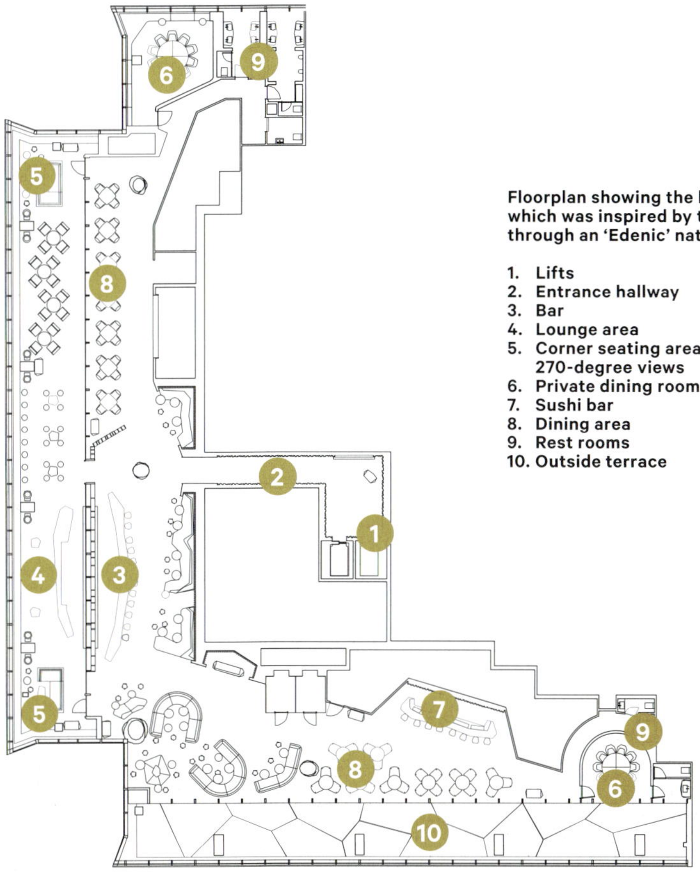

Floorplan showing the layout of Ozone, which was inspired by the idea of a walk through an 'Edenic' natural environment.

1. Lifts
2. Entrance hallway
3. Bar
4. Lounge area
5. Corner seating area with 270-degree views
6. Private dining room
7. Sushi bar
8. Dining area
9. Rest rooms
10. Outside terrace

The sumptuous rest rooms continue the marble theme.

Instead of trees, Katayama's Eden features a forest of quirky, curving columns, finished in high-gloss white.

'The project was possible only because it's in Hong Kong'

Ozone

Location Ritz-Carlton, 118/F,International Commerce Centre, 1 Austin Road West, Kowloon, Hong Kong
Design Wonderwall (wonder-wall.com)
Client Harbour Vantage Management Ltd
Materials Marble, marble inlay, polished stainless steel, Corian, Corian mesh,solid ebony, gold metal, yellow onyx, glassfibre reinforced gypsum (GRG)
Furniture Custom-made
Flooring Custom-made Voronoi patterned carpet; ebony inlay Voronoi patterned flooring; artificial timber Voronoi-patterned flooring
Lighting Custom-made glass sphere pendant lights; chandeliers by Flos; ripple lighting system in silicon oil tank; LED lighting with colour control system; LED indirect lighting with effect control system
Area 755.3 m²
Completed May 2011

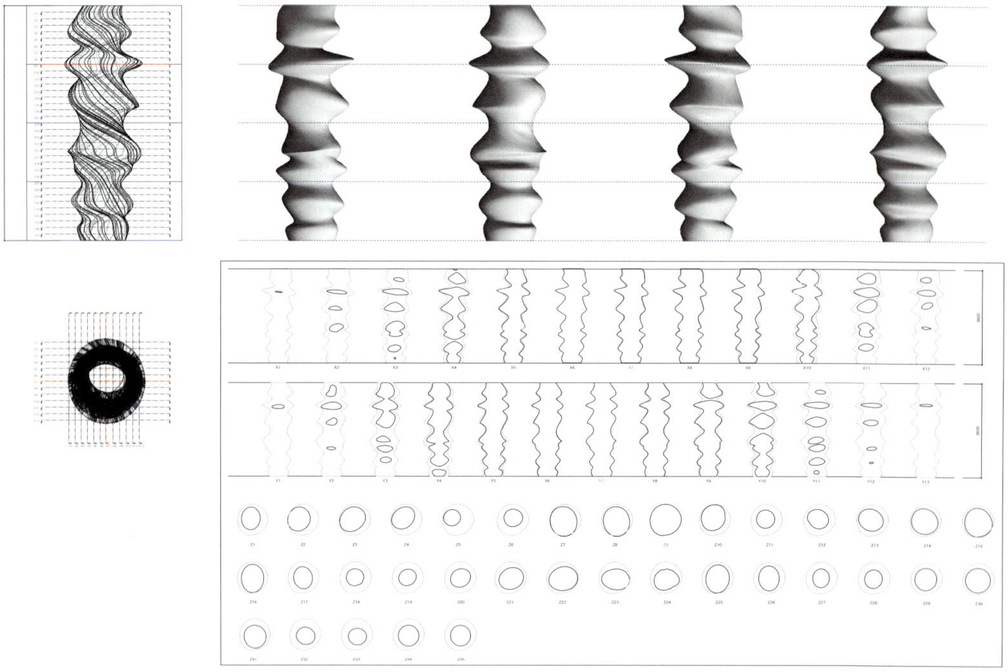

Computer modelling produced the series of sinuous columns.

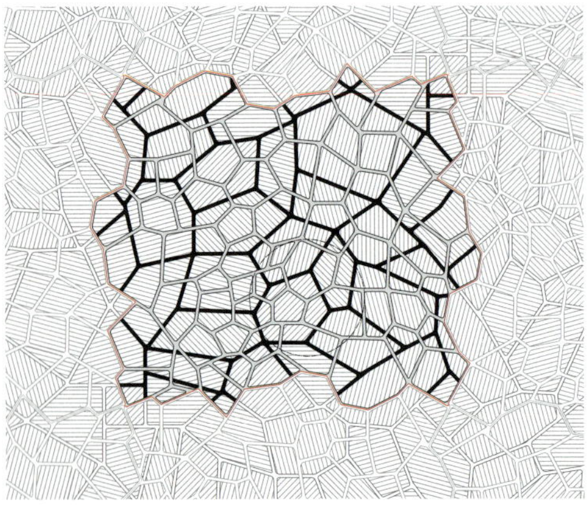

Voronoi diagrams provided the geometric blueprint for much of the basic ceiling design.

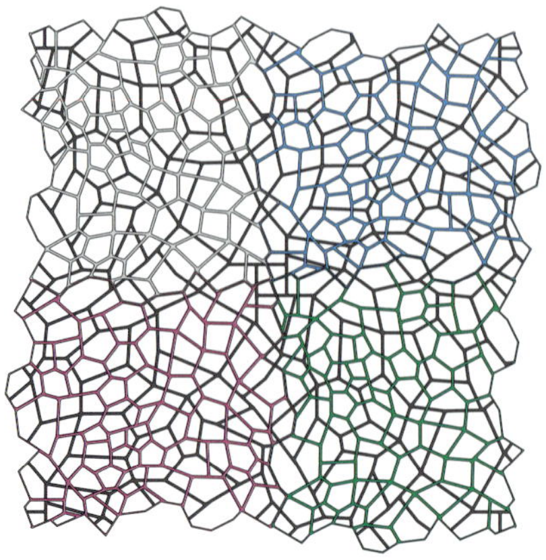

Layered over each other, the Voronoi screens add texture and complexity to the ceiling.

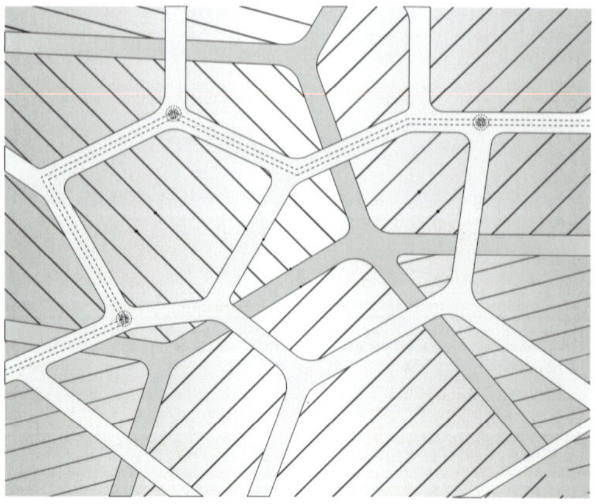

Diagram showing the contrasting layers of the Voronoi ceiling screens.

The Entertainer

Words **Kanae Hasegawa**

In designing Ozone, Wonderwall's idiosyncratic Masamichi Katayama aimed for 'electric, not relaxing, luxury'.

As Hong Kong's GDP grew by 7 per cent last year, the city's buildings continued rising to new heights as well. Occupying the top floor of Hong Kong's recently opened ICC, Ozone is the highest restaurant and bar in the universe – and probably the closest to heaven a diner can get. If 'having your feet on the ground' means being sensible and realistic, visiting Ozone catapults you into another, less prosaic reality. Here, you are high above ground and surrounded by the extraordinary.

You'd think that Japanese designer Masamichi Katayama, founder of Wonderwall, would not be overly impressed by the commission for Ozone – such is his success that he's currently working on 25 upcoming projects. But he was thrilled to be asked to design this space in Kowloon, which is one of Hong Kong's most breathtaking locations. 'I was thoroughly excited about designing a space that commands such an outstanding view of the city,' he says. 'The project was possible only because it's in Hong Kong. To prevent the space being overwhelmed by the energy of the city, the design called for luxury at its most extreme.' When you're 490 m above ground level, your normal state of mind ceases to exist – a great advantage for a man who has said he likes using design to access the subconscious. For Ozone, Katayama came up with a concept he calls 'Edenic Experiment', in which he envisioned a world of naturally inspired idealized forms filled with a sense of wonder. With that in mind, he went on to create a phenomenal entertainment venue.

Masamichi Katayama of Wonderwall.
Photo courtesy of Wonderwall

Guests encounter an enchanting environment that exceeds human imagination – a rare experience for a clientele that includes Hong Kong's business elite. For those who have studied abroad, travelled widely and amassed the means to buy anything they like, the ultimate luxury may indeed be an experience far beyond the realm of expectation. For that reason, Katayama intentionally abandoned the Ritz-Carlton's style of Asian Art Deco so familiar to Hong Kong's wealthy. 'I envisaged Ozone as electric, rather than relaxing, luxury,' he says of an interior that reflects the dynamism of the city.

Within the space, the designer laid out bar, lounge, dining and terrace areas, loosely connecting them by means of a passageway surrounded by an array of columns that evoke trees growing in the Garden of Eden. Voronoi tessellation on the floors imitates light filtering through a leafy canopy, while echoing the pattern of branches along the passageway. It was a challenge for Katayama, whose idea of luxury is 'less is more', to craft this 'unimaginable' space. 'It was an experiment for me as well,' he says, 'and, actually, it was a pleasure to be able to think so far outside the box.' These days, 80 per cent of Katayama's portfolio consists of projects overseas. 'Hong Kong is very much a cosmopolitan city,' he says. 'The clientele is diverse, with many different tastes and backgrounds. I was able to bring my full experience of working with international clients to this project. I must admit, however, that the setting – the location – was really the best material you could put into the design of Ozone.'

Are You Experienced? *Five Recent Wonderwall Projects*

Photos **Kozo Takayama**

Super A Market, Aoyama, Tokyo, 2011
Multi-brand luxury items are presented in what Masamichi Katayama calls a 'supermarket environment'.

Nike, Harajuku, Tokyo, 2010
A shoe chandelier and waffle sole-patterned walls are among the whimsical details of this playful palace for sports megabrand Nike.

Pass the Baton, Omotesando, 2010
A stacked and layered approach demonstrates the principle of 'form is action', while boosting the identity of a Japanese brand that recycles used goods, including vintage treasures.

A-Factory, Aomori, 2010
A market, a cider factory, a restaurant and cafés occupy the A-Factory complex, which is close to the Shin-Aomori bullet-train station. The area is known for its apples, and this lively space is devoted to the process of making apple cider.

I.T Hysan One, Hong Kong, 2011
Katayama designed the building as well as an interior that radiates a sense of constant change, thanks to multiple stores on every floor.

Staat designed the House of the Purple façade. The main entrance is quite a distance from the street.

No Place Like Home

An oasis surrounded by the hustle and bustle of the city is House of the Purple's inner courtyard and its verdant vertical garden.

Words **Femke de Wild**
Photos **Kasia Gatkowska, courtesy of Staat**

Behind Staat's House of the Purple is a branding concept for a South Korean credit-card colossus.

The interior design of House of the Purple is based on the idea of visiting a good friend at home. The 'living room' – or lounge and club area – is a glossy environment highlighted by objects such as Amanda Levete's gleaming black Drift Bench (centre).

The interior features a carefully selected mix of classic designs, contemporary pieces and custom-made objects, such as the lamps above the bar.

What a surprising combination: a relatively small Amsterdam-based agency and Korea's second largest credit-card company, Hyundai Card. Nonetheless, it was creative outfit Staat – officially called ...,staat – that captured the commission for the design of an exclusive club for the financial giant, a venue accessible only to Hyundai Card's 20,000 Purple cardholders; unless you've ascended to the company's Black status, you can't get classier than this. In a stringently designed office in Amsterdam, Staat creative director and partner Jochem Leegstra, strategy director and partner Michiel Steyn, and 3D designer Pepijn Smit join me at a sizable conference table. As I am about to learn, the concept for the Hyundai Card business lounge is the product of an eight-member team of designers, copywriters and strategists, who viewed the project as a branding exercise.

How did you get the job?
Michiel Steyn: In 2010 we were in Seoul – initially for another project – when we, along with several international interior-design companies, were invited to enter a competition for the design of a business club for Hyundai Card's Purple cardholders. This is a company that uses design to communicate its brand at all levels: the cards themselves, the office space, the ads – even the art on the wall. Although the competition centred on interior design, we never interpreted it as such. We used branding as a line of approach in our pitch and the location as a tool. Our proposal included not only an interior but the creation of an entire world, from a name – House of the Purple – to a menu, a logo, staff uniforms and everything online.

How do you approach an interior from the viewpoint of branding?
Steyn: We started by looking at where the brand wanted to go. We felt that our client, CEO Ted Chung, wanted the brand to have a warmer image and, at the same time, an air of exclusivity. So we asked ourselves: what's warmer and more special than a night out at a restaurant or a club? What is it that money can't buy? The answer: friends and taste. The club had to be the home of a friend who welcomes you into his world of art, food, wine and music. A place that transforms the cardholder from a client into a friend.
Jochem Leegstra: We adopted that perspective, and we won the pitch. We did more than just suggest a certain type of lamp or sofa for the interior. The lounge became a living room, the restaurant a kitchen, the terrace a garden and the toilet a powder room. And we were more like curators than designers.

Curators? In what way?
Pepijn Smit: The idea emerged from seeing the club as a home rather than a house. When you visit someone, you don't walk into a place that's furnished in a single style. It's always an eclectic collection of stuff that's been accumulated down through the years. So we became collectors – of furniture, art, books, lamps and even the materials we used for purpose-made objects. We collaborated with designers like Marcel Wanders and Richard Hutten on special objects, and we worked with Humans Since 1982 on a unique model of their Clock Clock. All custom-made furniture began in our studio as drawings and was manufactured later by Fiction Factory in Amsterdam.

Are those special objects for sale? That's something you see hotels doing more and more often.
Steyn: We considered the sales angle, but 'taste is not for sale' was at the heart of our concept. Chung found it unnecessary. Club members are already Hyundai Card customers; he didn't like the idea of profiting even more in this way. When we get to phase two of the project, the roll-out will include products you can buy online. We've been discussing the upcoming phase with potential partners like Comme des Garçons and *Monocle*. ...

‘Physical spaces are gaining in importance as a branding tool’

Two artists known as Humans Since 1982 made a special model of their Clock Clock for House of the Purple. The object looks like a digital timepiece but is actually an analogue clock.

Classic designs and works of art appear throughout the interior. On the table is a radio designed by Dieter Rams.

30-45

The Black card is a serious corporate card for CEOs; the Purple card targets creative entrepreneurs and independent business people between the ages of 30 and 45.

House of the Purple

Location Seoul, South Korea
Design ..., staat creative agency (staatamsterdam.nl)
Client Hyundai Card (hyundaicard.com)
Furniture Vintage and contemporary pieces by Dieter Rams, Jaime Hayon, Myoung Ho Lee, Paul Smith, Richard Hutten, Piet Hein Eek, Marcel Wanders, Humans Since 1982 and others; curated by Staat
Custom-made furniture and lighting Designed by Staat, produced by Fiction Factory
Lighting plan Light and Shade Lighting Consultants, Seoul
Vertical garden Hak & Associates, Seoul
Interior and exterior fabrication Kesson, in cooperation with SEL Interior Design
Project coordination Hyundai Card project team; Mr Oh and Mr Vlessing (Total Impact, Seoul)
Area 300 m^2
Completed April 2011

House of the Purple was conceived as a domestic space – the ‘home of a friend’ – furnished with designer classics and objects crafted especially for the project. Staat made a mood board for each room.

After learning of their popularity in Korea, Staat had gaming tables made for the restaurant area of the club. The red sculpture in the right corner is Heart, by Nathan Sawaya.

... You mentioned Hyundai Card's focus on design. Did you integrate the concern's corporate identity into the club interior?
Leegstra: Not literally. You may notice a subtle use of purple, but we purposely avoided going to extremes. The concept is based on a mind-set, not on form or design. It's the overall sense of quality – with a strong focus on materials – that corresponds to the style of Hyundai Card. The entrance area is a chromed tunnel with lilac-grey curtains, black-lacquered furniture and smoky mirrors. The garden is an oasis of green, and we selected cognac-coloured leather for the custom-made accessories. We could have gone for gold taps in the rest rooms as well, but we rejected the idea. It's not about money – it's about value.

Have you carried that sense of quality through on other levels?
Leegstra: When you go to a friend's house, you browse his bookshelves, you eat what comes out of his kitchen, you drink the wine that he's chosen. Asians understand the ins and outs of such a notion. They lured a sommelier away from a wine bar, a man with the gift of gab, who encourages guests to taste various vintages. And they have a good barista working there, who makes a perfect cup of coffee and serves it with a little brass spoon. Not a detail has been overlooked.

Staat was founded in 2000. What made you start doing interiors in 2004?
Leegstra: When Heineken asked whether we could design a bar, we said yes. It seemed like a logical step to me. I'm not an architect, but I do tend to think in terms of spatial environments, whether I'm designing an event or a pop-up store or a club. We've got a staff of 25 at Staat, including designers and someone who does renderings. We can create images of anything and everything.
Steyn: We're interested in communicating ideas. It might be through a logo, a corporate image, an interior – or through a combination of forms. We're being asked more and more often to come up with a total package.

Doesn't all this attention on interiors clash with the rapid increase of all things virtual in today's world?
Steyn: But that's precisely why physical spaces are gaining in importance as a branding tool. In addition to the online world, we need real locations with a heart. And television is on the decline when it comes to advertising. We need new media to convey information – and interiors are one solution. You can even use an interior to combat scarcity. Good workers are hard to find, and a well-designed interior is a way to offer people something extra. _

Staat had vintage chicken-wire glass flown from New York to Amsterdam with which to make room dividers; the completed screens were then transported to Seoul.

20,000

... of those with a Hyundai Card have a Purple card. The number of Black cardholders is approximately 2000.

Ted Chung, CEO of Hyundai Card.

A Deck of Cards

Established in 2001, Hyundai Card has evolved into South Korea's second largest credit-card company, with more than 9.5 million cardholders. At the head of the firm is CEO Ted Chung. Hyundai Card issues no fewer than 23 types of cards, which vary from cards with a low daily spending limit to the premium Black card. The in-house design lab employs about 15 people. The corporate image – sleek and chic – is reflected throughout the organization, including in the art and design pieces commissioned especially for Hyundai Card. The company produces sports and cultural events, such as concerts, and collaborates with Taschen Books, *Monocle* magazine and the Museum of Modern Art in New York. Eschewing the traditional hierarchical structure, Hyundai Card is an egalitarian organization. The company headquarters in Seoul overlook the Korean Parliament Building. Staff amenities include a gym, golf facility, laundry and shoeshine service, plus an extensive library.

-House *of*
the Purple

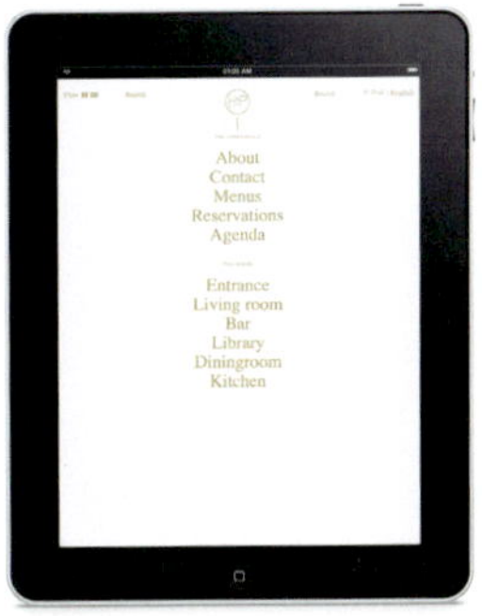

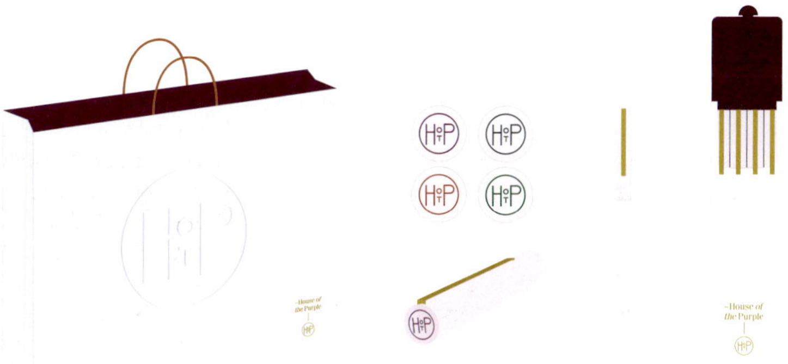

In addition to the interior, Staat created the company's corporate identity, the logo, a menu cover, staff uniforms and everything online – designs that feature a subtle use of purple, golden fonts and cognac-coloured leather.

Subtle Style

Seoul-based writer Matt Flemming checks out House of the Purple for *Frame*.

Although House of the Purple boasts a sleekly elegant entrance area, the club's interior is absolutely understated. Seoul's nightlife can be a sensory overload completely bereft of subtlety, but the genius of House of the Purple's curated design emerges bit by bit, as each piece of designer furniture, each lighting fixture and each curio makes its appearance. Items stand out yet fit into the overall aesthetic: a Tom Ford book in the café-kitchen library, an old-fashioned metal desk lamp in front of the bar, the silver magnificence of an Italian espresso machine, a small grey suitcase radio near the front window – not to mention novelties like art piece Clock Clock.

House of the Purple seeks to make you feel at home in a place where you know you're always welcome – where you're greeted with a free drink before sitting down in the kitchen for a game of chess, as you might be at the house of a friend – a friend who's evidently spent a lifetime assembling a collection of cool conversation pieces. It's a brilliantly executed theme, even if these rooms don't really feel like they're in a friend's house.

A decades-old, movie-theatre sound system plays jazz and classical music, setting a quiet, sophisticated mood. House of the Purple may not offer the Saturday-night stimuli that everyone's looking for, but the bartender does make an excellent martini.

1

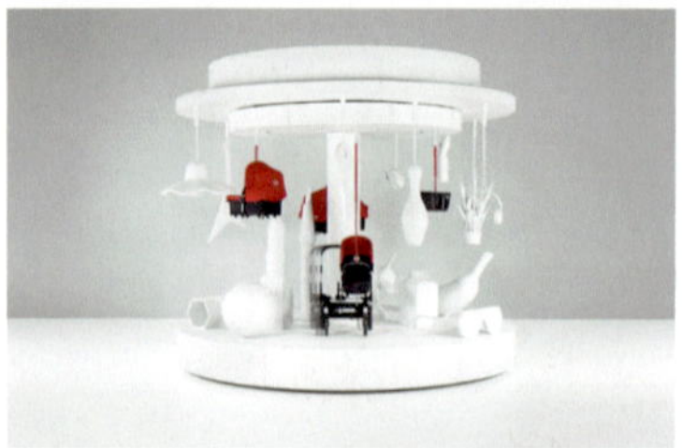
2

3

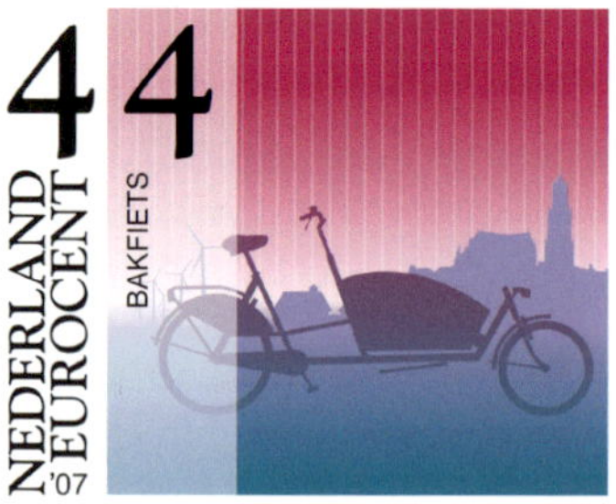

4

Building Brands
7 Staat Clients

***Lucas Bols*, 2006-ongoing (1)**
Corporate identity, brand strategy, product design, glassware, packaging, communication tools, retail spaces

***Bugaboo*, 2002-ongoing (2)**
Corporate identity, brand strategy, communication tools, campaigns, art direction

***Heineken International*, 2002-ongoing**
Art direction, design, packaging, communication, campaigns, HQ portfolio bar

***Nike EMEA*, 2002-ongoing**
Concept, design, art direction, retail campaigns, communication tools, retail environments, pop-up stores

***Wrangler Blue Bell*, 2009 (3)**
Concept, art direction, design, look book

***Converse*, 2008**
Global design direction, retail communication, trade-fair stands, events

***TNT Stamps*, 2007 (4)**
Design

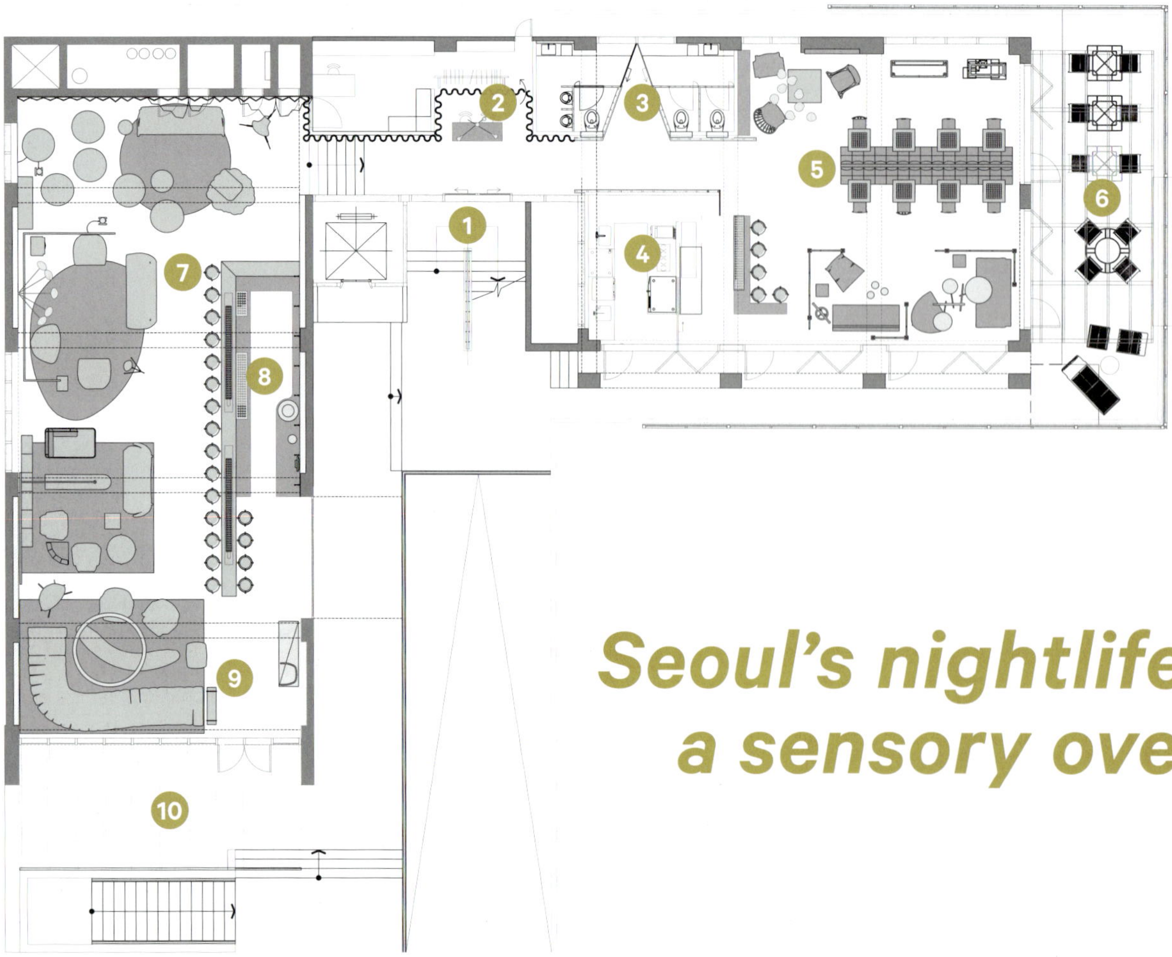

Floorplan.

1. Entrance
2. Front desk
3. Rest rooms / powder rooms
4. Kitchen
5. Restaurant
6. Garden
7. Lounge / living area
8. Bar
9. Space for a stage
10. Façade

Seoul's nightlife can be a sensory overload

In the rest rooms, Staat used mirrors, a window and diagonally positioned doors to produce a kaleidoscopic effect.

OPTUS
ANZ

Diamond in the Rough

Both inside and out, the Myer department store in Melbourne is a jaunty jewel in the mid-city monotony.

Words **Penny Craswell**
Photos **John Gollings**

One of the building's more dramatic features is its gold-metal and glass roof, which can be seen from surrounding buildings.

Completely re-imagined, the Lonsdale Street façade is now a puzzle of orange, grey and white triangles.

At Myer Bourke Street, escalators – which are often hidden rather than highlighted in retail interiors – are a striking element of the swirling central atrium.

Parts of the interior feature the same triangular pattern used on the façade.

Myer Bourke Street

Location 314-336 Bourke Street, Melbourne, Australia
Design NH Architecture (nharchitecture.net)
Client Colonial First State Global Asset Management
Materials Exterior: custom-coloured composite aluminium, performance glass, powder-coated steel, Brighton Light precast concrete. Interior: glass, composite aluminium, painted plasterboard, mirrored acrylic resin, stainless steel, rendered concrete, Australian hardwood. Roof: custom-coloured HH Robertson Boldrib
Lighting NDY (ndy.com)
Flooring De Fazio (defazio.com.au), Melbourne parquetry timber floors
Walls Concept Ceilings, Comcraft, Custom Ceilings (customceilings.com.au)
Area 47,000 m²
Costs €163.5 million
Budget €220 million
Completed December 2010

A vast, cleverly angled atrium in white rises to meet a diamond-shaped skylight at the Myer department store in Melbourne. Designed by NH Architecture, both atrium and gleaming overhead glazing are central features of the firm's rejuvenation of one of the city's iconic buildings. Russian émigré Sidney Myer established the store in Melbourne's main street in 1914. Over the course of his life, Myer acquired and amalgamated several adjacent buildings, and by the time he died in 1935 the department store had become central to the lives of Melburnians, who eagerly awaited Christmas window displays and began salivating as they neared the food hall. Myer's empire continued to flourish after his death, and stores bearing his name can now be found throughout Australia.

The original Bourke Street building welcomed additions over the years, but before NH's intervention the results were a hodgepodge of outdated interiors, with no dynamic circulation plan and a severe lack of natural light. As part of one extremely outrageous scheme, the eighth-floor windows were blacked out completely. Perhaps Myer's most significant features, dating to the 1930s, are an Art-Deco façade on Bourke Street and Mural Hall, a space housing a significant collection of murals depicting the achievements of women through the ages (the paintings are the work of Australian artist Napier Waller). When Myer and Colonial First State commissioned NH to renovate the building, the architects began by restoring the heritage-listed façade and Mural Hall.

Whereas retail floors on the Bourke Street side were easy to tackle, the back of the building was a warren of awkward levels and ceiling heights. During their pitch, the architects suggested demolishing this section of the building. Myer's response was that if the store committed to a partial demolition and a rebuild – as opposed to a simple renovation – the architects had better make it worthwhile. Robert Nelson of NH was in total agreement: 'If you are going to invest that kind of money, the project has to be as interesting in ten years' time as it is on opening day. The place should be uplifting and inspiring.'

NH accepted the challenge, choosing to frame the heritage features in contemporary architecture rather than merely restoring them. The 1930s façade on Bourke Street was redone in gleaming white and the Lonsdale Street façade re-imagined completely as a puzzle of orange, grey and white triangles. ...

The architects created an optical illusion that makes the floors below, when viewed from the top level, seem larger than they are.

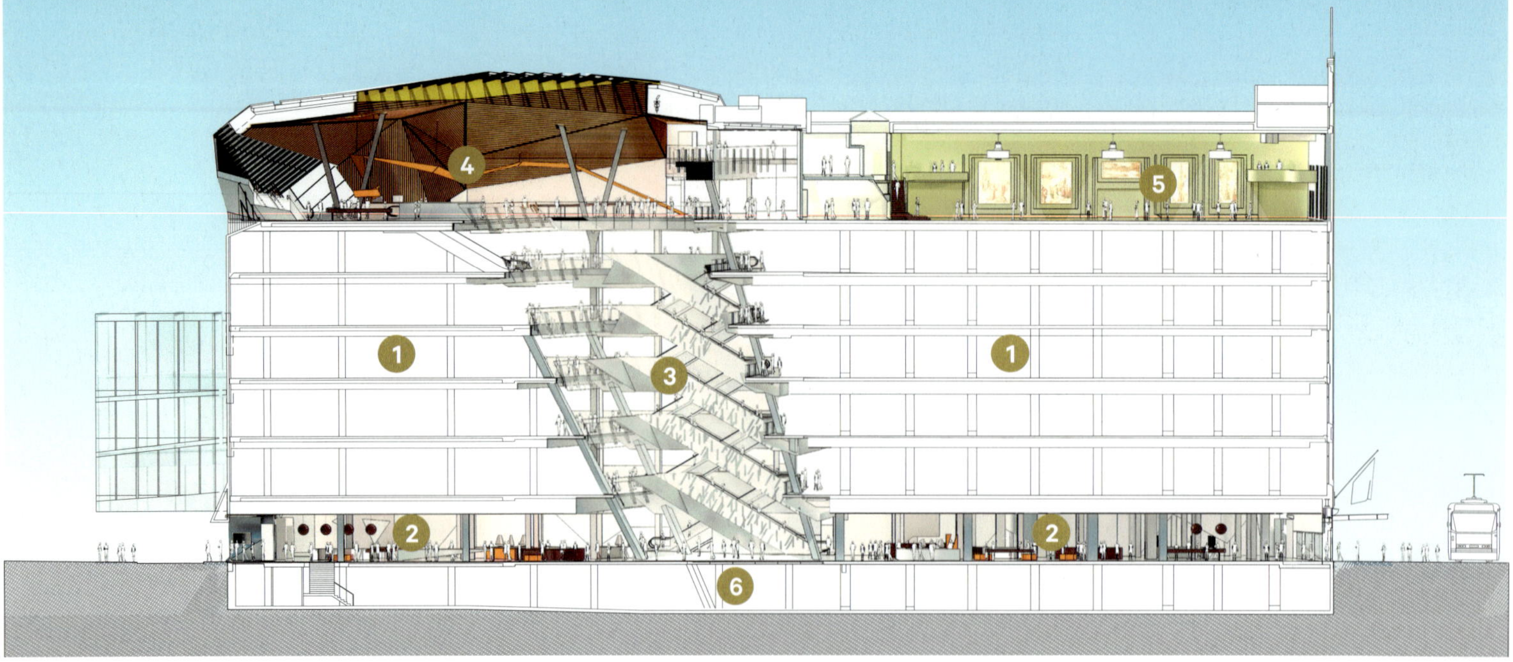

Long section.

1. Retail area
2. Ground-level retail area
3. Atrium
4. Event space
5. Mural Hall
6. Basement

'The project has to be just as interesting 10 years from now'

... The shape continues to the roof, where a spectacle of gold-metal and glass – best seen from surrounding buildings or Google Earth – presides.

On the top level of the store, Mural Hall remains intact yet is brought into the here and now through the surrounding contemporary architecture. Reinstated as a space for hosting functions, the hall is coupled with an adjacent pre-event area. A timber-banded ceiling complements triangular and diamond-shaped skylights and windows in the Art-Deco style.

The most remarkable transformation, however, is that of the atrium. As most customers enter the building from the south, NH opted for an atrium with a slight north-facing incline, which provides shoppers on the ground floor with dramatic overhead views. The atrium flares out, becoming wider at each level and creating a monumental, airy atmosphere. The skylight at the summit of the escalator illuminates the space; on sunny days, beams of light dance on dozens of glossy surfaces.

Aware of how often escalators are jammed into a building with no thought of how unsightly they might be, NH used white side cladding for the moving stairs. White – the colour of choice for floor, ceiling and walkways – is combined with elements in glass, aluminium and other silver-coloured materials. 'We wanted to make more out of the escalators by giving them the ceremonial nature of a grand staircase,' says Nelson. 'The structure was subordinate and slipped into a ribbon-like expression that winds its way up, as if someone's peeled an orange in a continuous strip and pulled on it.'

Even though the architecture is not continuous, shoppers on the ground floor sometimes find themselves standing on a 'sweet spot' that makes them feel as though the entire structure has lined up to form a perpetual spiral. Those at the top looking down experience an optical illusion caused by a play of scale. Gazing into the void below, they see each floor appearing larger than it actually is and, because of the tapering design, are permitted a glimpse of what's at each level. 'It's called "persistence of vision" or "mental mapping",' says Nelson. 'It's about perspectival tricks and the psychology of design. Being in command of what you're doing allows you to do some wonderful things.' Besides dramatic views of the interior, the top floor offers impressive vistas of Melbourne through windows much larger than those normally found in retail establishments.

Department stores can be difficult to design. It's often a struggle to entice customers to enter, let alone to explore the upper levels. Because the popularity of department stores as one-stop-shops is threatened by the onset of online retail, something extra is needed to draw clients into a bricks-and-mortar emporium. Myer is proof that architects can meet the challenge by transforming shopping destinations into monumental marvels capable of redefining city centres. _

On the top level, a ceiling banded in timber incorporates Art Deco-inspired skylights.

Asian Fusion

The Mandarin Oriental gets a signal dash of French flavour.

Words **Chris Scott**
Photos **Hélène Hilaire**

Heidi Winge Strøm's fabric is draped and folded on the walls of Sur Mesure to create 'a wall covering that winks at the world of Parisian *haute couture*'.

The palette was inspired by the hotel's oasis-like garden

We begin outside the doors of the Mandarin Oriental. The high-end hotel group has just opened its first French location on the prestigious Rue Saint-Honoré in Paris. By inviting several designers to participate in the creation of new destinations, the hotel group has assumed the role of curator. Here in Paris, hidden within the 1930s architecture renovated by Jean-Michel Wilmotte and the opulent interiors of Sybille de Margerie are an elegant bar and two restaurants designed by Jouin Manku Studio.

French-born Patrick Jouin and Sanjit Manku, an English-speaking Canadian of Indian origin, seem to be the perfect fit for such a project. The arrival in Paris of an international hotel chain that's firmly tied to its oriental roots speaks clearly to designers like Jouin and Manku, who can imagine nothing better than balancing 'two creative worlds that listen to each other'. In developing a concept for a 21st-century oriental palace that would still be inherently Parisian, the designers focused on savoir-faire, or the know-how of a bygone era. They pictured a contemporary design informed by the expertise of traditional craftsmen and artisans – a space that would unravel like a journey, continually sparking the visitor's curiosity.

Inspiration struck the designers the moment they entered the majestic lobby and spotted the 455-m^2 oasis-like garden at the heart of the hotel. The work of landscape artists François Neveux and Bernard Rouyer, the verdant haven was to play a pivotal role in Jouin Manku Studio's design, in terms of both palette and the spatial relationship between inside and outside, especially since Patrick Jouin ID would be custom-designing both indoor and outdoor furniture for the project.

The interior journey begins in Bar 8, a mysterious grotto where colours and textures echo garden foliage. In this dimly lit den, low tables are dotted with tiny lights and glistening beams make their way in from the garden outside. While these lights may *appear* to shine like gems, one wall in the bar literally does. Lit from below, a panel inlaid with hundreds of dazzling Lalique crystals is reflected in the bronzed ceiling. Jouin and Manku – who invariably aim for a synthesis of old and new – also designed the monumental central bar. Cut from a 9-tonne block of marble, the bar travelled through Europe before reaching the hotel. Extracted from a quarry near the Spanish city of Seville, the block was transported to Carrara, Italy, to be sculpted and finished before being shipped to its final destination, where the floor required reinforcement to support its weight. When asked why they couldn't have used resin to make the bar, the designers say they like using 'living' materials and call the bar 'a touch of history'.

An oversized glass door lends access to the second destination. Sur Mesure is far more than a restaurant: it's a total gourmet experience. The striking interior enhances the diner's culinary pleasure rather than diverting attention from the food. According to Manku, 'Three-star restaurants don't often put people at ease. These "food temples" can become too stifling. Sur Mesure's contemporary setting has a comfy, slip-off-your-shoes kind of vibe. We were lucky enough to have input from the restaurant's distinguished and innovative chef, Thierry Mark. He's a fellow aesthete with an eye for detail.'

The design for Sur Mesure began with simple white cotton, a material 'so familiar that it's part of our daily lives', ...

In the rest rooms, petal-shaped tiles on the walls produce a brilliant display of colour.

Wall panels in the Camélia restaurant
resemble flower petals.

Bar 8, Sur Mesure, Camélia and Jardin

Location Mandarin Oriental, 251 Rue Saint-Honoré, 75001 Paris, France
Design Jouin Manku Studio (patrickjouin.com)
Client Société Foncière Lyonnaise (fonciere-lyonnaise.com)
Furniture Cassina (cassina.com), Laval, Cinna
Lighting DPA (dpalighting.com)
Area 685 m² (interiors), 220 m² (courtyard)
Completed June 2011

Jouin Manku Studio

... says Manku. 'We liked the idea of doing something extraordinary with something we see all the time.' The walls and ceiling are draped with textile designer Heidi Winge Strøm's flame-retardant fabric, Trevira CS. 'Here I see the textile, which has to fulfil several functions, as a cross between spatial solution and clothing,' says Winge Strøm. 'It's both a wall covering and a wink to the world of Parisian *haute couture.*' Pure-cotton napkins and jacquard-woven cotton tablecloths designed by Winge Strøm, together with menus printed on exquisite Japanese rice paper, further complement an evening of fine dining at Sur Mesure. Serving as a focal point, a light well featuring an elliptical crystal structure completes a scene devoted to the senses.

A stroll through the garden takes visitors to Camélia, an all-day restaurant and breakfast room whose name refers to the fragrant blossoms that grace the garden in the summer. Rue Saint-Honoré may be famous for fashion, but it's also a hotspot for patisseries. Following suit, Camélia boasts a cake counter with tempting treats displayed in wooden alcoves. The walnut counter – its shape echoing that of the marble volume in Bar 8 – forms the centrepiece of Camélia, which can be seen as a continuation of the garden. Nature floats in and out of its doors, with tile floors giving way to wooden surfaces and lamps seeming to sprout from rugs. Jouin and Manku, who are critical of over-furnished restaurants that end up looking like showrooms, developed the intriguing rug-cum-lamp to reduce clutter.

As the brand name suggests, the hotel's interiors combine natural elements with oriental influences. Jouin Manku Studio, however, approached the project as one distinctly anchored to its environment. 'We wanted these spaces to provide unique, radical experiences that bring out the beautiful emotion that is Paris,' concludes Manku. 'It's not about the décor but about a specific type of energy – a vibration that makes the hairs on the back of your neck stand up.' _

Camélia boasts a cake counter with tempting treats displayed in walnut alcoves.

'Three-star restaurants don't often put people at ease'

'The fabric is a wink to the world of Parisian haute couture'

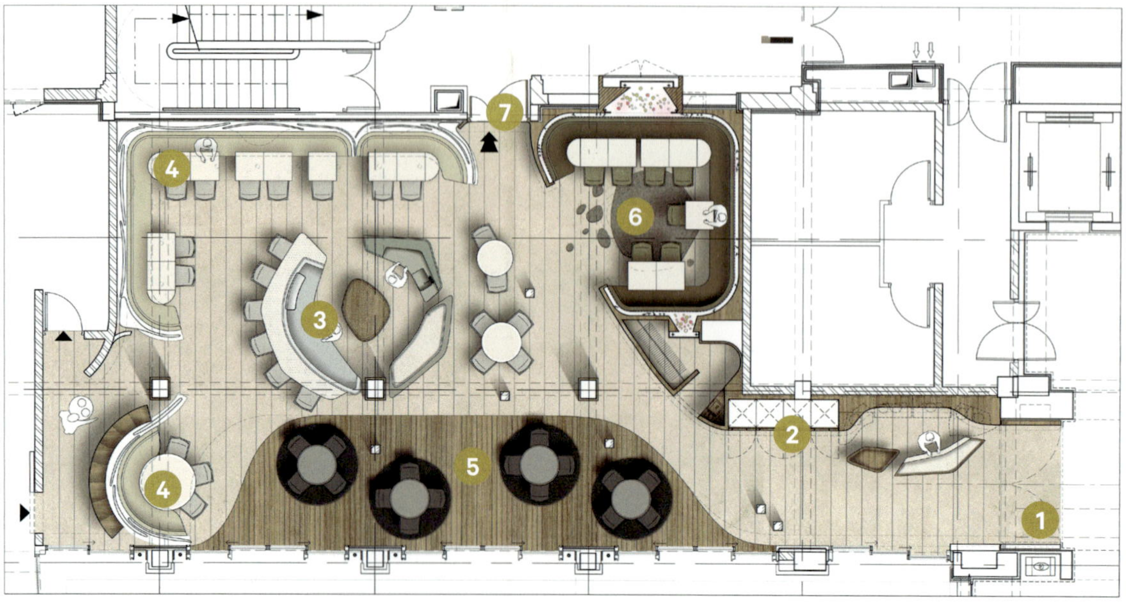

Plan of Camélia restaurant.

1. Entrance
2. Cake counter
3. Live Asian cooking counter
4. Dining alcove with 'petal' panels
5. Contrasting wood-floored area
6. Separate dining space
7. Exit to dining terrace

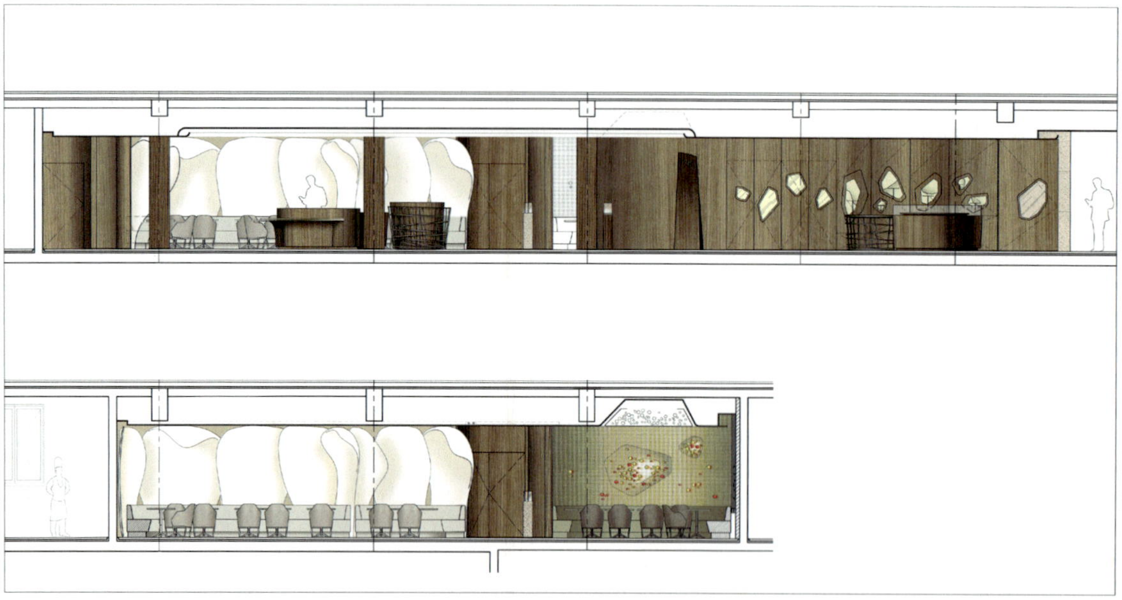

Elevation of Camélia restaurant, showing the contrasting walnut-wood panelling and fabric petal panels.

Initial drawings of custom-designed furniture for Camélia.

The walnut display counter forms the centrepiece of Camélia.

Reports

150
Showroom Sets
Gaggenau

Showroom

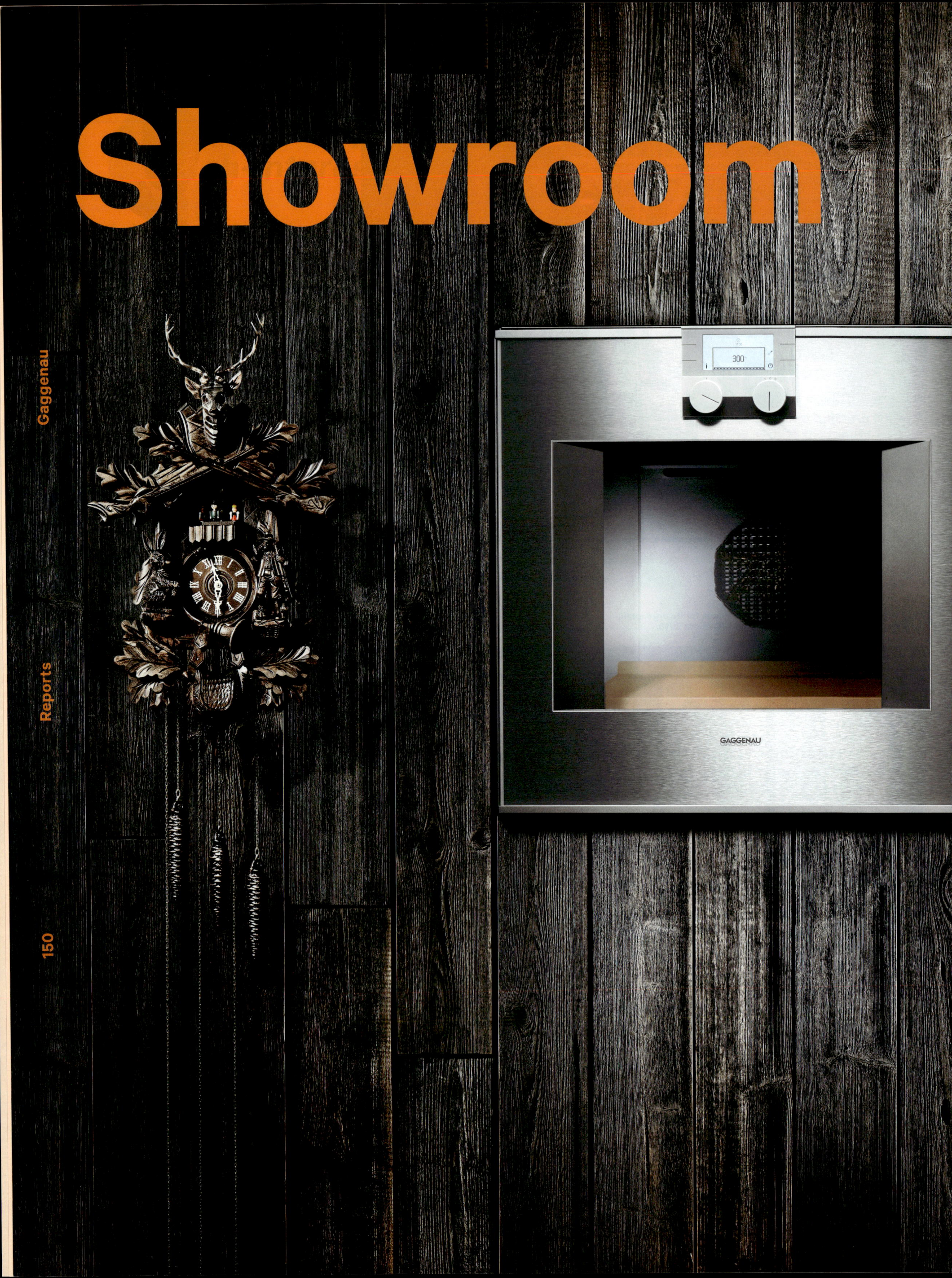

Strategems

Gaggenau's new Amsterdam flagship is the latest in a global series.

‘We don’t want an exhibition of home appliances’

Showrooms are an integral part of the brand experience, says head of Gaggenau International Sven Schnee.

Sven Schnee.

You're about to open a showroom in the Netherlands. Why now?
Sven Schnee: The Netherlands is a design-driven, lifestyle-oriented market, which matches our brand identity well. Amsterdam is also an international hub for architecture and culture and, therefore, an important lever for Gaggenau to upscale even further.

The showroom will be in Hoofddorp, approximately 20 km from Amsterdam. Why did you choose this location?
We wanted a new, Cradle to Cradle building. This means all the materials used during construction can be recycled into other materials or returned to the environment. The philosophy extends to the completed building, too. We need to use as much daylight as possible in the organization of workspaces and to minimize energy and water consumption. This particular design was more suited to an environment just beyond the area's main city.

Istanbul is home to one of Gaggenau's more recently opened high-rise showrooms.

'Underlining the importance of quality is paramount for any luxury brand'

How many showrooms do you have?
We have more than 15 flagship showrooms worldwide. They're situated in high-rises (in Shanghai, Beijing and Istanbul, for example), in city centres (Paris, London, Hangzhou, Dubai) and in business areas (Singapore, Stockholm, Amsterdam, Irvine). The choice of location depends on the targeted operating strategy for the market.

What do they look like?
Our showrooms reflect both culinary culture and an exclusive lifestyle. Instead of merely showcasing an exhibition of home appliances, we want potential customers to experience the emotional and educational aspects of Gaggenau. We hope this approach will foster long-term customer-product relationships.

While our spaces are quite open – merging dining, lounging and cooking – we can still control various zones to create privacy when needed. This flexible concept means our branded architecture is easily implemented in showrooms of different sizes – from 80 to 300 m², or more.

How do you cope with the different scales?
In each showroom we establish three distinct zones – live cooking, dining and lounge/wine bar – and have a heritage wall for displaying information about our past in terms of brand evolution, milestones, product innovation and communication. The live cooking and dining spaces form the core of each showroom. We fit the lounge and heritage wall around these elements to create a homogenous whole. Our larger showrooms also display an exploded model of a Gaggenau oven door.

Are the showrooms designed in-house?
For the last four years our design and marketing departments have worked in close collaboration with eins:33, a Munich-based architecture firm, to design all our showrooms, mobile kitchens, virtual showrooms and trade-fair stands. Because eins:33 fully understands our brand DNA – uncompromising, extraordinary and authentic – the environments they develop match our company values.

These values extend to our entire brand experience, including advertising, website and events. Everything needs to be authentic and to convey the same message. Underlining the importance of quality is paramount for any luxury brand. We really want our claim – 'The difference is Gaggenau.' – to ring true for our customers. _

Gaggenau

Website gaggenau.com
Locations Headquarters in Munich; key production facilities in Germany, France, Spain and Turkey
Established 1683 (as an ironworks in Gaggenau, Germany)
Number of employees More than 500 worldwide, including 50 in R&D
Area of distribution Worldwide in over 40 countries
Most important market Germany
Market sector Luxury kitchen appliances
Best-known product 90-cm-wide oven EB 300
Bestselling product 200 series oven

Photo Alexei Tylevich

196
Back to the Futurist
Luigi Colani

Photo courtesy of Philips

192
Replicating Revolution
3D Printing

Sven Schnee.

You're about to open a showroom in the Netherlands. Why now?
Sven Schnee: The Netherlands is a design-driven, lifestyle-oriented market, which matches our brand identity well. Amsterdam is also an international hub for architecture and culture and, therefore, an important lever for Gaggenau to upscale even further.

The showroom will be in Hoofddorp, approximately 20 km from Amsterdam. Why did you choose this location?
We wanted a new, Cradle to Cradle building. This means all the materials used during construction can be recycled into other materials or returned to the environment. The philosophy extends to the completed building, too. We need to use as much daylight as possible in the organization of workspaces and to minimize energy and water consumption. This particular design was more suited to an environment just beyond the area's main city.

How many showrooms do you have?
We have more than 15 flagship showrooms worldwide. They're situated in high-rises (in Shanghai, Beijing and Istanbul, for example), in city centres (Paris, London, Hangzhou, Dubai) and in business areas (Singapore, Stockholm, Amsterdam, Irvine). The choice of location depends on the targeted operating strategy for the market.

What do they look like?
Our showrooms reflect both culinary culture and an exclusive lifestyle. Instead of merely showcasing an exhibition of home appliances, we want potential customers to experience the emotional and educational aspects of Gaggenau. We hope this approach will foster long-term customer-product relationships.

While our spaces are quite open – merging dining, lounging and cooking – we can still control various zones to create privacy when needed. This flexible concept means our branded architecture is easily implemented in showrooms of different sizes – from 80 to 300 m^2, or more.

How do you cope with the different scales?
In each showroom we establish three distinct zones – live cooking, dining and lounge/wine bar – and have a heritage wall for displaying information about our past in terms of brand evolution, milestones, product innovation and communication. The live cooking and dining spaces form the core of each showroom. We fit the lounge and heritage wall around these elements to create a homogenous whole. Our larger showrooms also display an exploded model of a Gaggenau oven door.

Are the showrooms designed in-house?
For the last four years our design and marketing departments have worked in close collaboration with eins:33, a Munich-based architecture firm, to design all our showrooms, mobile kitchens, virtual showrooms and trade-fair stands. Because eins:33 fully understands our brand DNA – uncompromising, extraordinary and authentic – the environments they develop match our company values.

These values extend to our entire brand experience, including advertising, website and events. Everything needs to be authentic and to convey the same message. Underlining the importance of quality is paramount for any luxury brand. We really want our claim – 'The difference is Gaggenau.' – to ring true for our customers. _

'Underlining the importance of quality is paramount for any luxury brand'

Istanbul is home to one of Gaggenau's more recently opened high-rise showrooms.

Gaggenau

Website gaggenau.com
Locations Headquarters in Munich; key production facilities in Germany, France, Spain and Turkey
Established 1683 (as an ironworks in Gaggenau, Germany)
Number of employees More than 500 worldwide, including 50 in R&D
Area of distribution Worldwide in over 40 countries
Most important market Germany
Market sector Luxury kitchen appliances
Best-known product 90-cm-wide oven EB 300
Bestselling product 200 series oven

Cooking Up Ideas

Head of design Sven Baacke talks trends and strategies – and explains how he stays ahead of the game.

Sven Baacke.

What are you currently working on?
We work two to four years in advance, so unfortunately I can't give anything away just yet . . .

Surely you can discuss Gaggenau's new releases . . .
This year we launched CX 480, a full-service induction cooktop. You can place things freely anywhere on the surface, and CX 480 recognizes the size and shape. It caters for anything from a large teppan-yaki plate to a small coffeepot. It's a restful, unobtrusive design that hides just how technical this product really is.
A TFT touch-panel display shows exactly where items have been placed. Users love the interaction involved.

If you work so far in advance, does the market change even before your designs are released?
It's about staying ahead of the game. As Henry Ford is alleged to have said: 'If I were going to give people what they wanted, I would have invented a faster horse.' It's hard to envision the future, but we take cues from what's happening around us. A Gaggenau appliance isn't like a mobile phone; it should be visually and technologically up to date for at least a decade or two.

What's your strategy?
We do a lot of research with international chefs, and our team is full of foodies. We follow blogs on design, architecture and art and make sure we're present at the major design fairs in Milan and New York. It's not just about what's going on in the creative world but also about how people are developing and changing. Using our research, we sketch ideas and discuss them with technicians who have the expertise to transform them into new technologies.

Gaggenau defines its values as 'authentic, extraordinary and uncompromising'. How do your products reflect this?
When I joined Gaggenau in 2003, someone noted that I was entering the white-goods industry, but I don't see Gaggenau as a typical manufacturer of white goods. Our values mean we don't use fake materials or decorative patterns that may go out of style. We're always looking for the best design solutions, we believe functionality is beauty, and we try to infuse kitchen appliances with soul, while making them durable and technologically advanced. A Gaggenau kitchen is a statement.

What materials do you use?
Historically, appliances were made from durable steel – a throwback to the professional kitchen. We use steel, but we incorporate aluminium, brass, cast iron and glass as well. All our materials are authentic and pure; we don't use imitations. We want long-lasting materials that age well, like a leather bag. Even with scratches and signs of use, the products still look good – sometimes even better.

How are products developed and tested?
Consumer demand drives a lot of our work. Some of our ideas are a bit far-fetched. Technicians have been known to walk out of the room saying, 'Oh my god . . . we can't do that!' In all seriousness, though, we have great relationships with the technicians. We work very closely with one another. Design isn't an afterthought to technology, or vice versa. We're not here just to prettify things.

What are consumers demanding right now?
The current trend is for kitchens to be more integrated into the home. It's a social place, where certain things should be displayed rather than hidden. We often enjoy a glass of wine in the living room, so why should drinks be stored in the kitchen? If we start making these kinds of changes, spaces and products will have to look different, too.
The various areas should be more integrated, meaning architects, kitchen designers and appliance manufacturers should all work together. People are also demanding energy-efficient appliances. We're looking at ventilation issues, including possibilities for re-circulating air inside rather than pumping it outdoors. These are things we need to work through with architects and planners.
As technologies develop, we're figuring out how to give technical products more soul. Working with user interaction and new interfaces is more than just putting an iPad on an oven.

Gaggenau's appliances follow an avant-garde philosophy. What does this mean to you?
I like to think of it as *traditional* avant-garde. Gaggenau is over 300 years old, and our original pieces were avant-garde. Some of our ovens from the 1960s still look modern today. We're traditional and heritage-oriented yet innovative. We set benchmarks with technology, and we're ahead of our time yet fundamentally true to ourselves. Some of our customers with 30-year-old ovens have said they don't need to replace their appliances just because they're going out of style.

Have you considered re-releasing classics?
It has been a topic of discussion. We still have some special items – a 90-cm-wide oven designed 25 years ago, for example – that are difficult to change, but we don't want to be retro. A Gaggenau product won't be the next Volkswagen Beetle; we don't want to reinvent the past. _

Factor of Four

1 **Which designers do you follow?**
Most recently I've been focusing on *what's* going on, not *who's* making it happen. I read blogs to keep up to date with changes in the design world.

2 **Is there a product you wish you had made?**
Something completely different to an appliance, like a Caterpillar [bulldozer] or a flower shop.

3 **And a product you're glad you didn't make?**
To be honest, no. But I can't predict the future. I've designed things that I wish had been made but weren't for various reasons.

4 **Who are your main competitors?**
There are, of course, other kitchen brands that we compete with in the market, but we have such a distinctive range of products that if you want Gaggenau, you'll probably buy Gaggenau. It's like the desire to have a specific brand of car.

Products

Adopting the traditions of functional German design, Gaggenau designs appliances as statement pieces. The essence of the brand's character is its constant evolution of the past, coupled with a willingness to break conventions and to pursue innovative visions. With a philosophy that designer Sven Baacke describes as 'traditional avant-garde', Gaggenau strives to stay ahead of the times. The philosophy extends to the principles that drive specific designs: authenticity, sculpturalism, prominence and capaciousness.

Gaggenau appliances can be combined to form various configurations. Shown here are the CM 250 fully automatic espresso machine (middle), the BM 275 Combi-microwave oven (left) and the BS 254 Combi-steam oven (right).

CX 480, a full-surface induction cooktop, with AL 400 telescopic table ventilation. AL 400 will be available from December 2011.

The Vario cooling 400 series allows for any number of flexible arrangements, such as an RF 463 freezer (mid-left) and an RC 462 refrigerator (mid-right), flanked on either side by an RW 414 wine-climate cabinet with temperature control.

Putting on the Style

Gaggenau hallmarks are found in a handful of key elements that encompasses heritage, location, size, colour and a tightknit group of reliable partners.

A showcase displaying the numerous layers that make up the door of a Gaggenau oven is included in some of the larger showrooms.

Heritage

Using wood sourced from the Black Forest, home to the town of Gaggenau where the kitchen brand began, Gaggenau inserts a 'heritage wall' into each showroom. The wall displays images and objects – vintage components, documents and photographs – that hark back to the company's early years.

The heritage wall in Istanbul's newly opened showroom.

Detail of the Istanbul heritage wall.

A rubber stamp from the former Gaggenau headquarters.

The staff of the Gaggenau ironworks, 1916.

Three models of coal- and gas-fired stoves that were produced from the late 19th century until well into the 20th century.

A showroom's 'heritage wall' harks back to the company's early years

The Istanbul showroom offers a breathtaking view of the city from the 32nd floor of its high-rise accommodation.

Paris

Rather than following a standard floor plan or using the same type of ceiling in every showroom, eins:33 treats each project individually, paying special attention to location. When using a listed building, as they did in Paris, the designers highlight the juxtaposition of old and new. Here, they focused on maintaining the level of detail present in internal doors, thus pointing up the contrast with Gaggenau's modern display system.

Gaggenau's intervention left the traditional residential entrance of the Paris showroom intact.

Online Showroom

Gaggenau launched its virtual showroom in 2010. Visitors begin the journey in the Gobi Desert, where a trio of cubes provides portals to three very different locations: a New York City loft, a Balinese pagoda and a Venetian palazzo. Within each setting, visitors are free to express their creativity, configuring and interchanging appliances as desired.

Each setting has a set of characteristics applicable to real-life residential environments. The New York interior is generous in size, while the Balinese pagoda helps visitors combine natural materials with the aluminium surfaces of Gaggenau appliances to produce a harmonious whole. In the Venetian residence, stainless-steel products enhance a period interior.

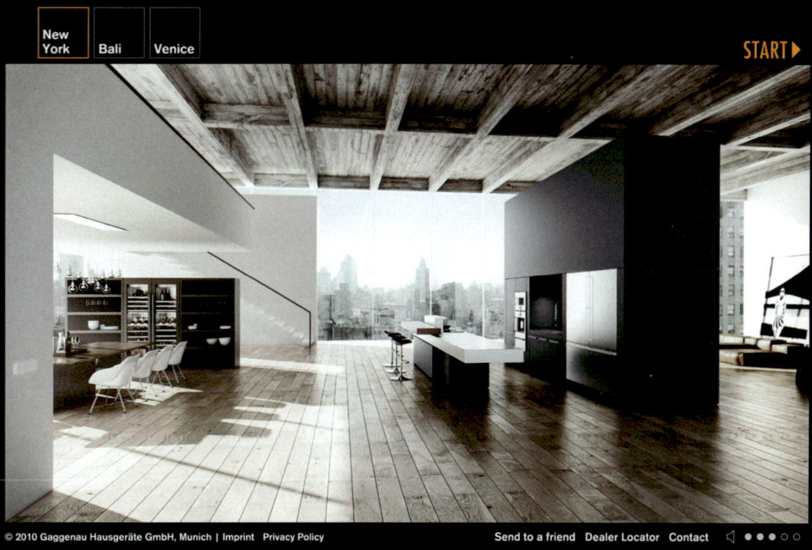

Visitors to the New York City cube take a lift to the 42nd floor, where they enter a loft and become acquainted with the technical specifications of different products.

The Venetian cube reveals the contrast between functional Gaggenau products and traditional interior details.

Set in lush surroundings, the Balinese pagoda shows how natural materials and aluminium surfaces can work in harmony.

Size

With so many showrooms of various sizes, Gaggenau has a list of basic elements that appear in all spaces. Additional features depend on the site, the specifications and the operating concept. In each showroom, you find Gaggenau appliances, of course, along with display furniture that both accommodates and contrasts with the products. Display units are usually dark and matte to offset the gleaming metal appliances. Large-scale colour photography of food is incorporated into all showrooms to complete the picture.

Other elements – which vary in size, according to the amount of space available – include one or more heritage walls displaying information on Gaggenau's origins, product evolution and craftsmanship; and local details that connect the showroom to its environment.

The 6-m² mobile kitchen is easy to transport – it fits into a few relatively small cases – and can be assembled in a matter of hours.

Mobile Concepts

Clients don't always have to visit one of Gaggenau's permanent showrooms; sometimes, the showroom comes to them. The company has two travelling concepts – a 6-m² mobile kitchen and a 44-m² mobile showroom – that allow the team to set up a Gaggenau centre almost anywhere, virtually overnight. As compactness is vital for transport, the showroom fits into a shipping container and the kitchen takes up just a few small travel cases.

Multibrand

Although only 44 m², the mobile showroom provides customers with the same emotive brand experience as the larger flagship showrooms yet fits into a shipping container for easy transport.

Colour

You can't get more contrast than black against white, a combination that clearly expresses Gaggenau's uncompromising nature and explains why all corporate communication is predominantly black and white. Selective use of orange and green breaks up the monochromatic scheme and helps consumers distinguish between 'warm' appliances, such as ovens, cooktops and ventilation systems, and 'cool' appliances for refrigeration, dishwashing and the like.

A showroom can be set up almost anywhere, virtually overnight

Orange and green – used as accents to underscore Gaggenau's core colours, black and white – appear in photos of food displayed throughout the relatively neutral showrooms.

Partners

Gaggenau's design and marketing departments work in close collaboration with eins:33, a Munich-based architecture firm, to design all showrooms, mobile kitchens, virtual showrooms and trade-fair stands.

In addition to Gaggenau products, showrooms display select merchandise from partner brands that help create a 'family home' atmosphere, reflecting the lifestyle of target customers. In line with Gaggenau's desire to put a strong emphasis on local design and manufacturing, all brands have German roots and are chosen for their long, successful histories. Appearing in each showroom are Walter Knoll soft seating, Occhio lights, architectural lighting solutions by Erco, Bang & Olufsen audio and video systems, and objects by Zwiesel 1872 and Meissen. 'Our partners share our DNA,' says head of Gaggenau International Sven Schnee. 'They all believe in quality and manual assembly. Approaching sales in a similar way, they focus on providing quality service and support. These brands are all niche players in luxury products available worldwide.'

eins:33

Originally established in Stuttgart in 1999, eins:33 was relaunched in Munich by Hendrik Müller in 2005. Since 2007, Müller has worked with associate partner Georg Thiersch to produce a wide range of architecture and design projects worldwide, including showrooms, exhibitions, large-scale office and residential developments, and smaller projects for private clients.

einszu33.com

Occhio

Occhio Divo may seem purely decorative, but – like Gaggenau's range of products – the lamp is extremely functional. Eight interchangeable reflective heads allow the user to direct light precisely where it's needed. Even without the extended history that marks Gaggenau, Occhio has a rapidly evolving success story that appeals to the kitchen brand.

occhio.de

Decorative and functional: Occhio Divo pendants provide work surfaces with

Erco's track-mounted Optec spotlights lend definition to Gaggenau showrooms.

Erco

Specialists in producing engineering hardware and software for architectural lighting, Erco provides track-mounted spots and wall-washers for Gaggenau showrooms. Certain spaces also incorporate Erco's ceiling-recessed luminaires. In the same way that Gaggenau hopes to offer an experience rather than simply selling a kitchen appliance, Erco believes in giving its customers light and not just lamps.

erco.com

A 'family home' atmosphere reflects the lifestyle of target customers

Walter Knoll's Living Landscape 730 can be configured to suit any number of spaces.

Walter Knoll

Each Gaggenau showroom exhibits the same style, yet certain factors – such as size and location – demonstrate the value of a flexible system. Walter Knoll's Living Landscape 730, designed by EOOS, adapts to various situations thanks to sides and back that can change positions. With a minimalist design that echoes the Gaggenau aesthetic, PearsonLloyd's Turtle bar stools provide seating at higher counters. With a history dating back to 1865, Walter Knoll is a well-established German manufacturer.

walterknoll.de

... brand is well developed now, so it's a good time to promote it strongly. The new ad campaign I mentioned will feature photographs by Andrea Ferrari.

How does Flexform Mood affect your mainline Flexform brand?
They are two completely different worlds.

Why pick Shanghai and New York for your latest showrooms?
Shanghai is an important centre of rapid economic development. New York is a challenge: one that we're facing with courage. It's important for our brand image that we're there, and we have a really good partner to manage our showroom. We've also created the Flexform NY company. It will manage the local side of things better than our Italian office could do, because it's on the ground.

Exports make up 75 per cent of sales

In the age of the computer, how important are physical showrooms for you?
Very. Walking into a showroom is like walking into someone's home. You get to know the inhabitants better when you see where they live. For us, a physical presence is as important as a digital presence.

Flexform is a family firm in a global, corporatist age. What advantages and challenges does that have?
Our biggest strength is that our company is run by two generations – one older, one younger. Together we confront and complete each other. _

Factor of Four

1 How has the way that Flexform communicates its brand changed?
Matteo Galimberti: We have always believed passionately in communication. Back in the 1970s, this prompted Flexform to invest boldly in brand design by the great graphic designer Pino Tovaglia – who also designed the Pirelli brand – and in advertising in the world's best publications. The image of our advertising campaigns – handled for 30 years now by Natalia Corbetta – is very cohesive and recognizable and has remained consistent over time. We always use black-and-white photographs against which the red branding stands out – images featuring sophisticated environments that frame a single character. The photographs are always by exceptional photographers: Aldo Ballo, Gabriele Basilico, Maria Vittoria Backhaus and, today, Gianni Berengo Gardin.

2 Which manufacturers do you work with?
Ones that are extremely local – all production occurs within a radius of 3 km. Every Flexform product is made locally, in Italy, which facilitates our extensive quality-control procedures. Of course, production costs are higher, but the payoff is finer quality and better craftsmanship, thanks to our highly specialized workers.

3 Which designers do you follow?
No external designers at the moment. For Flexform, it continues to be Antonio Citterio, who is currently the leader among architects designing upholstered products. For Flexform Mood, on the other hand, we are continually seeking fresh stimuli and input from different designers, and we're happy with the recent work of Roberto Lazzeroni.

4 Tell us the difference between Flexform and Flexform Mood.
Flexform started out as a manufacturer of upholstered products – sofas and armchairs, essentially – with three key values: elegance, high quality and comfort. Over time we added coffee tables, bookcases and furnishing accessories. With Flexform Mood, we have a more complete collection in the international style covering a number of environments: living room, day zone, dining zone, night zone.

Cestone chaise longue: probably Flexform's most technically challenging product.

Guscioalto, a new Flexform chair designed by Antonio Citterio.

Mood Man

Award-winning designer Roberto Lazzeroni is art director of the Flexform Mood brand.

What resources do you rely on to communicate the Flexform Mood brand?
Concepts such as elegance, luxury, special working processes, the importance of materials. They serve to create an atmosphere, the 'mood' of the brand. All this – and the products themselves – must be communicated with emotion.

How have you put your own stamp on the brand?
My natural predisposition to work with luxurious materials and to pay attention to details has been amplified and gratified by designing the Flexform Mood collection. I feel a real connection with it.

How did you reflect Flexform brand values in the new showroom you designed in Shanghai?
With an extremely meticulous plan, using some elements that I have already tried and tested in design layouts for the Milan Salone.

Name the best thing about working for Flexform.
Freedom with projects. And their highly developed technical capacity – we're talking skilled handcrafting in an industrial structure. I also value the friendly rapport that we've established.

How does the new Flexform Mood ad campaign develop the brand?
With a very exciting image that tells a little story about an interior. It's almost like a frame from a film.

Your ultimate ambition for the Flexform Mood brand?
For it to be loved by more people. _

Chair Charisma
Most Famous Products

ABC by Antonio Citterio.

Tube by Joe Colombo.

Ad Appeal

1969 Tube chair by Joe Colombo. Graphic design by Pino Tovaglia.

1985 Nonnamari by Antonio Citterio. Photography by Maria Vittoria Backhaus.

1996 Status by Antonio Citterio. Photography by Maria Vittoria Backhaus.

2011 Soft Dream by Antonio Citterio. Photography by Gianni Berengo Gardin.

Catalogue

Flooring

1

4

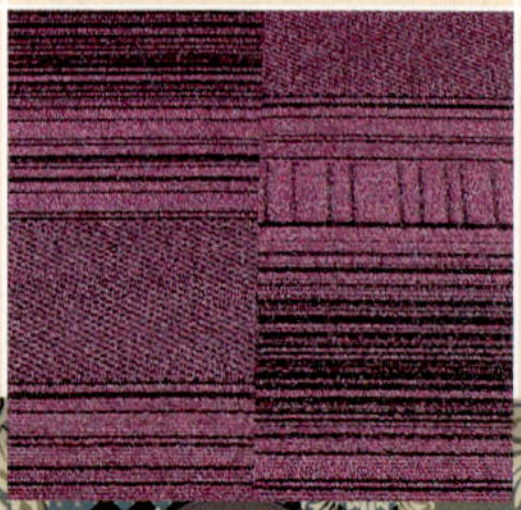
7

3

2

5

6

8

1. Oscar Worthy
by Bentley Prince Street

Old Hollywood comes alive with a contemporary interpretation of the 1940s in the form of flooring.

bentleyprincestreet.com

2. In-Groove
by Modulyss

Capture and retain dust particles more efficiently with carpet tiles that actually improve indoor air quality.

modulyss.com

3. Black Art Vulcano
by Object Carpet

You won't get stuck treading on this dark surface, despite a pattern reminiscent of rings made by pebbles tossed into a pool of tar.

object-carpet.com

4. Dolce Vita
by Tretford

Expressing a passion for life is Dolce Vita, whose 12 new colours emphasize comfort and quality in a cashmere-and-wool blend.

tretford.eu

5. Vintage Ornate
by InterfaceFLOR

This environmentally conscious carpet takes inspiration from heritage and history, making 'lived in' look new.

interfaceflor.com

6. Artisan
by Bolon

Opportunities are around every corner with Artisan, a textile-enhanced carpet available in standard rolls, tiles and unique design combinations through the Bolon StudioTM concept.

bolon.com

7. Urban Knit
by Todd van der Kruik for Milliken

No need to run for cover as Todd van der Kruik explores the trending practice of 'yarn bombing' to embellish a carpet tile using 45%-55% recycled content.

millikencarpet.com

8. Bodice
by Muurbloem for Ege

Layers of patterns and colours merge to create bold, fashion-influenced 'floorwear' by Muurbloem.

egecarpet.com

10

9

12

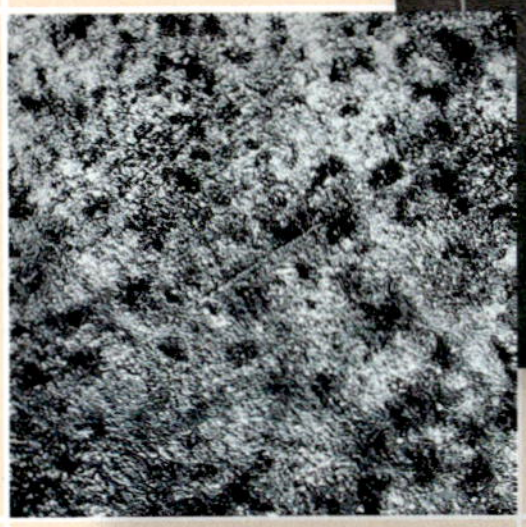
11

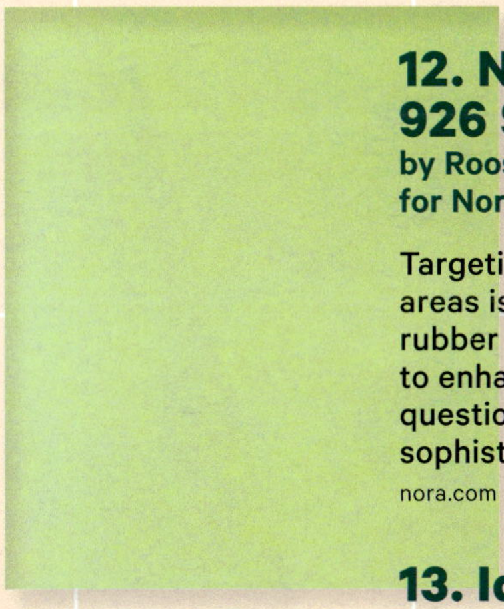
15

14

13

17

16

18

19

9. Edition 1
by Ross Lovegrove for Parador

When Parador extended an invitation to prominent designers, Ross Lovegrove conjured up laminate flooring with biomorphic patterns covering a circuit board for the feet.

parador.de

10. Materia
by Gaya Fores

The Materia tile – available in neutral shades of white, grey or black – adds a note of unobtrusive quality to today's bright interior spaces.

gayafores.es

11. Faux
by Nathan Allan

A floor tile designed with a swirling sandstorm pattern complete with a trademark 'glass sandpaper' finish, Faux provides a firm grip to any shoe tread.

nathanallan.com

12. Norament 926 Serra
by Roos en Ros for Nora

Targeting heavily trafficked areas is Nora's slip-resistant rubber flooring, which promises to enhance the interior in question with structured sophistication.

nora.com

13. Ideo Antique Flooring
by Jirachai Tangkijngamwong for Deesawat

Available in black, green, grey, purple and pink, Ideo imbues its surroundings with an intimate and honest air of rusticity.

deesawat.com

14. HeartOak
by Dinesen

Dinesen's uniquely authentic plank flooring reveals secrets hidden at the very heart of the oak tree.

dinesen.com

15. Unexpected Nature
by Forbo

Marmoleum is given new life in a flooring collection of rich hues and soft pastels composed of 97% natural raw materials (67% harvestable and 37% overall recycled content).

forbo-flooring.com

16. Deck
by Çanakkale Seramik

Add aesthetic depth to an indoor or outdoor space with tiles that have the appearance of wood.

kale.com.tr

17. Essenze Rare
by GranitiFiandre

Playing with streaks, shadows and shades is a tile that celebrates a feast of olive, black oak and cherry wood.

granitifiandre.com

18. Carving Grunge I.
by Mafi

Brushed and finished in white oil is a floor that not only finds inspiration in the Seattle music scene, but also showcases your favourite lyrics, sayings or designs.

mafi.at

19. Black American Walnut, Hand Scraped Face
by Ebony and Co

Hand-scraped floorboards finished in a texture akin to warped wood deliver a unique twist to a modern, practical product.

ebonyandco.com

1. Lake Como
**by Greg Natale
for Designer Rugs**

Swim through a modern lake of geometric motifs with Greg Natale's custom-coloured creation.

designerrugs.com.au

2. Dice Play
**by m-ar (R.J. Morganti)
for Paola Lenti**

Visions bouncing between Paola Lenti and Renato Morganti resulted in a playful display of dots on a die.

paolalenti.com

3. Zig Zag
**by Sebastian Wrong
for Established & Sons**

Finding your way across a hand-knotted rug with varying densities and heights that mimic the hills and valleys of a topographic map is . . . fun!

establishedandsons.com

4. Avenue
**by Ritva Puotila
for Woodnotes**

Brass, gold and green occupy the eyes of those who relax on a symmetrically striped carpet created for Woodnotes.

woodnotes.fi

5. Minore
by Hanna Korvela

Minore – a hand-woven mingling of soft wool and paper yarn – unites flooring and nature in stunning simplicity.

hannakorvela.fi

6. Fragment
**by Pudelskern
for Stepevi**

Creative minds Nina Mair, Georg Öhler and Horst Philipp have come together to produce a rug infused with the patina of antique objects.

stepevi.com

7. Beiras Bloom
by Casalis

Hand-knotting techniques from the Beiras region of Portugal are modernized with a jute backing, customizable colours and a fringe option, resulting in a rug that is irrefutably European.

casalis.be

1

2

3

4

5

6

7

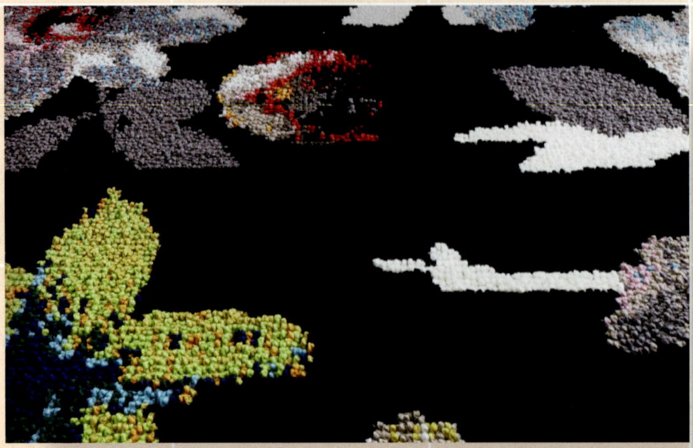

8

9

10

12

11

13

14

15

8. Figura
by Sahco

A coarse cotton base with a Panama weave supports an ornamental design that comes in two contrasting shades or makes a subtle tone-on-tone statement.

sahco.com

9. Bluhm
by Minotti

Hand-tufted virgin wool makes Bluhm a thick yet supple rug, which boasts a non-allergenic, non-slip, natural-latex underlay.

minotti.com

10. Losanges
by Ronan and Erwan Bouroullec for Nanimarquina

Rhombuses overwhelm in a handcrafted rug designed by the Bouroullecs and made by artisans in Northern Pakistan.

nanimarquina.com

11. Looping
by Hélène Dashorst for Limited Edition

Like a never-ending roll of ribbon, Looping is a maddening maze of moisture-resistant cord that takes more than 100 hours to compose.

le.be

12. Punto
by COR

A timeless design in New Zealand-wool and in a variety of colourways, Punto gives a contemporary feel to any interior space.

cor.de

13. Satura
by Alfredo Häberli for Ruckstuhl

Fine leather and buckles connect felt elements in a collage-inspired collection.

ruckstuhl.com

14. Alcaraz Sky
by Jan Kath

Referencing corrosion and eroded warehouses, Jan Kath's rug embraces his belief that 'perfection and smoothness are boring for our eyes'.

jan-kath.com

15. Fabric [Flat] Superdots
by Eva Langhans for Kymo

The Kymo lab has concocted a futuristic fabric that not only is soft and dirt resistant, but also features an anti-slip backing.

kymo.de

1. Steel
by Lorna Williams for Amtico

An addition to the Spacia collection is a rugged, masculine, metallic tile that breaks free from a typical matte surface.

amtico.com

2. Neocountry
by Apavisa

Simplicity and romance coalesce organically in Apavisa's tradition-based tile.

apavisa.com

3. Eco-Terr
by Ofer Mizrahi for Coverings ETC

A 70%-recycled marble and granite tile – available in polished, honed, sandblasted and antiqued finishes – Eco-Terr can be used for both floor and wall applications.

coveringsetc.com

4. Xeno Mosaic Polygon
by Agrob Buchtal

A dry-pressed ceramic tile, Xeno Mosaic Polygon transforms a simple space into a mesmerizing matrix.

agrob-buchtal.de

5. Beside
by Ghenos

In an unexpected turn, Ghenos uses the reverse side of a tile to showcase brightly glazed patterns of graphic lines.

ghenos.net

6. Tech
by Q-BO Project

Tech tile splits its personality between modern gloss and minimal matte.

q-bo-project.it

7. Area25
by Mosaico+ for Fabio Luciani

Area25 is made by grinding to a powder glass from waste and recycled products, a process that yields a solid, bright and environmentally friendly tile.

fabioluciani.it

8. Lefka
by Cerdomus Lab

A scenographic tile for walls or floors relies on digital technology and layering solutions for its impressive character.

cerdomus.net

9. Architecture
by Casalgrande Padana

Sophisticated and subdued matte surfaces capture contemporary elegance in indoor-outdoor stoneware.

casalgrandepadana.it

1

2

4

3

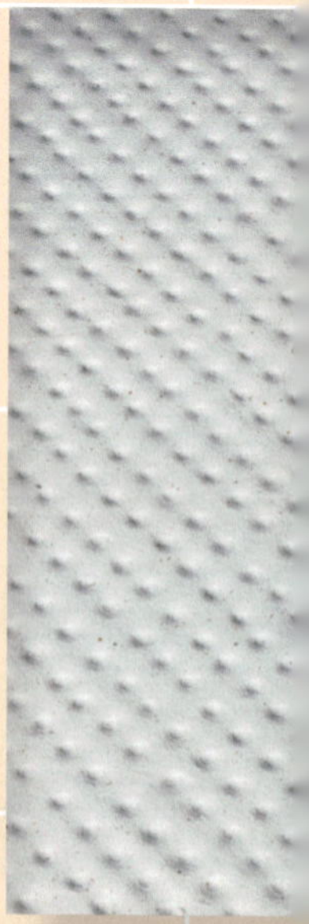

5

7

6

9

8

10

11

12

13

14

16

15

10. Terra Tones
by Royal Mosa

Exhibiting an unglazed surface and gentle earthy hues, the Terra Tones collection lives up to its name.

mosa.nl

11. Woodline Zebrano
by Vives Cerámica

Don't be fooled as Vives Cerámica disperses illusions of wood with its delusive collection of tiles.

vivesceramica.com

12. 1303
by PorcelaniteDos

What appears to be a slice of timber straight from the tree is a ceramic tile whose metallic wood finish is free of splinters.

porcelanitedos.es

13. Carbon
by Recer

Ideal for airports, gyms, hotels and high-traffic areas, this chemical-resistant tile, which comes in a range of formats and finishes, grants a top-notch performance.

recer.pt

14. Pico
by Ronan and Erwan Bouroullec for Mutina

Compacted particles of sand and minerals combine to produce a motif of recessed and elevated dots – on a matte surface of grey, sand, red or blue.

mutina.it

15. Lama
by TAU Cerámica

With a tactile touch that rivals natural wood, Lama offers aesthetic excitement to both indoor and outdoor surfaces.

tauceramica.com

16. Audrey
by Lea Ceramiche

Pastel shades within an elegant porcelain tile lend a light, contemporary feel to a diversity of interiors.

ceramichelea.it

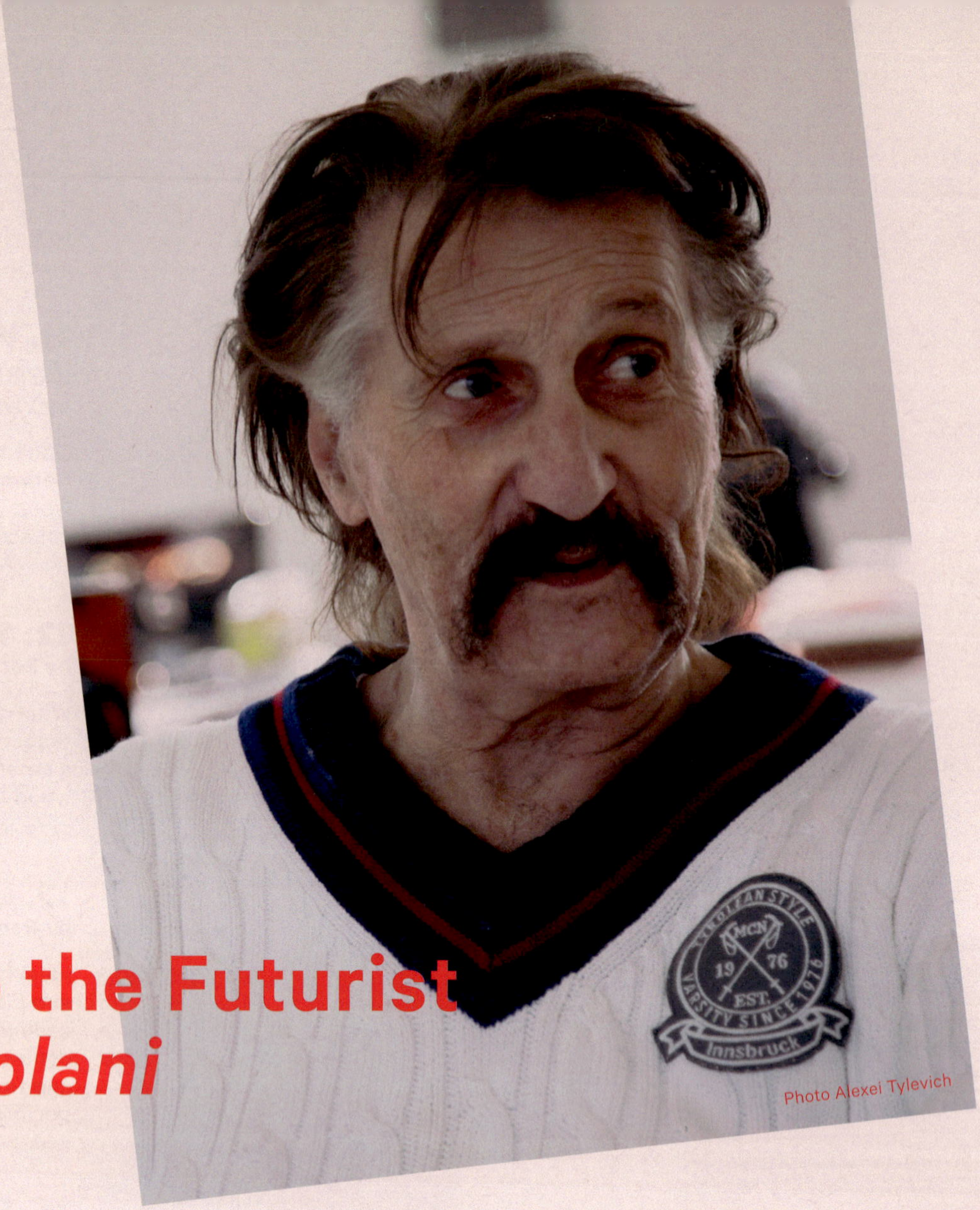

Photo Alexei Tylevich

196
Back to the Futurist
Luigi Colani

Photo courtesy of Philips

192
Replicating Revolution
3D Printing

Photo Petter Löfstedt

Goods

Tomorrow People

Graduates of European design academies explore materials, functions and techniques in pursuit of new and unexpected forms.

Words **Femke de Wild**

Aided by programmers, engineers and materials experts, Van Mourik developed a technique for integrating 3D-printed objects and fabric to produce a self-supporting object.

Voxel
by Elise van Mourik
Design Academy Eindhoven
The Netherlands
elisevanmourik.nl

'Voxel introduces a new application for 3D printing, fusing printed designs with textile surfaces. As a result, the textile becomes the end product; the mono-material body can stand on its own. I would like to contribute to the development of the "printing society" and to help discover and celebrate digital craft and open source design.'

3D Fabrics
Textiles as stand-alone products

Priyal Garg believes that Woven Dimension 3 can be developed for use in furniture, chandeliers, panels and installations.

Three-dimensional forms are woven on a hand dobby loom.

Woven Dimension 3
by Priyal Garg
Central Saint Martins, UK
priyalgarg.com

'My idea was to create forms that do not need manual or external treatment and are based solely on the craft of weaving. Commonly, 3D textiles are produced using fabric-manipulation techniques that rely on metal yarns, stitching or pleating. The aim was a process and form that make a relevant contribution to the practice of contemporary design.'

Although patterns are woven flat, the material assumes a structural form after removal from the loom.

Tak

by Boel Andersson
Konstfack, Sweden
boelandersson.com

'The ceiling forms a large part of the experience of a room, but is often forgotten. My project makes the ceiling the focus of attention. I created a complex, 3D structure by repeating one simple shape; the method I developed results in a three-dimensional material that can be industrially produced. The textile absorbs sound, spreads light and dramatically influences a space.'

Placed on an even surface, the fabric strips lie flat, but when they are separated and hung in the air, they have a voluminous, three-dimensional quality.
Photo Pär Hugosson

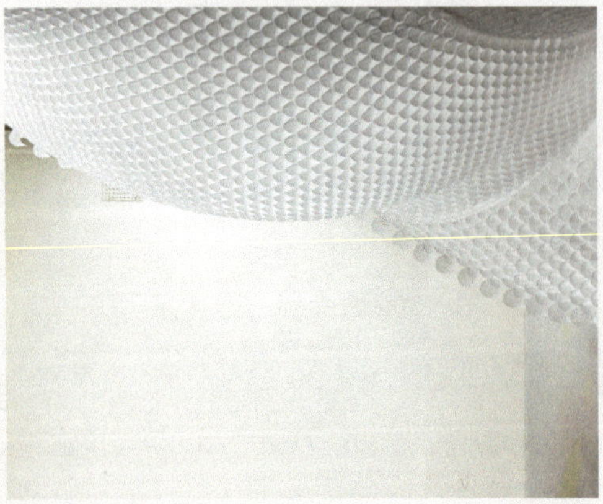

Boel Andersson's ceiling features scalloped, laser-cut strips made from a paper-like polyester.
Photos Petter Löfstedt

Using various materials and techniques, Ribul combines textile and air to make three-dimensional forms. She's recorded her experiments in photographs and videos.
Photo Lisa Holgersson

Air Momentum

by Miriam Ribul
Central Saint Martins, UK
miriamribul.com

'What I want to achieve is a connection between man-made constructions and nature. Although air has a natural impact that we can observe by looking at trees moving in the wind, it barely influences artificial constructions. The Air Momentum project is a collection of tools, materials and experiments that add an optical aspect to air. I believe that making air tangible is a way to enhance human interaction with the environment.'

Joint Benefits
Traditional carpentry transforms flat-pack furniture

Schindelholz's trio of lamps – another DIY kit – is based on a wood-joinery technique used in Japan to construct entire buildings.

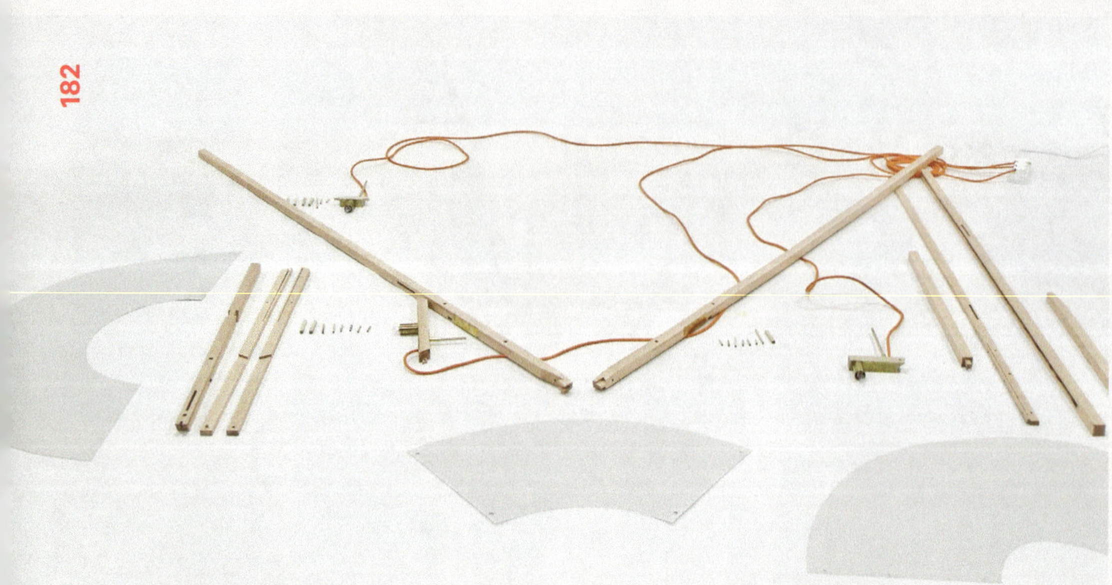

Joint
by Nicole Schindelholz
Design Academy Eindhoven
The Netherlands

'Japanese wood joinery is an amazing craft that takes a great deal of know-how, precision and patience. I want people to really experience this traditional technique. Joint is a series of three lamps that encourages people to assemble them using only their hands – and brains – no nails, no screws, no glue. My project is about more than function and user-friendliness; it's about thinking, feeling and experiencing.'

Photo Matthijs Rikken

Dowels
by Adrian Blanc
ÉCAL, Switzerland
adrianblanc.fr

'I am French, but I grew up in India, where I saw the work of many local artisans. I believe the future lies in a contemporary interpretation of "folk furniture". The ancient technique of barrel-making includes no glue, screws or nails. Two metal rings hold all the pieces together. I used this construction method to create basic furniture that can be assembled easily.'

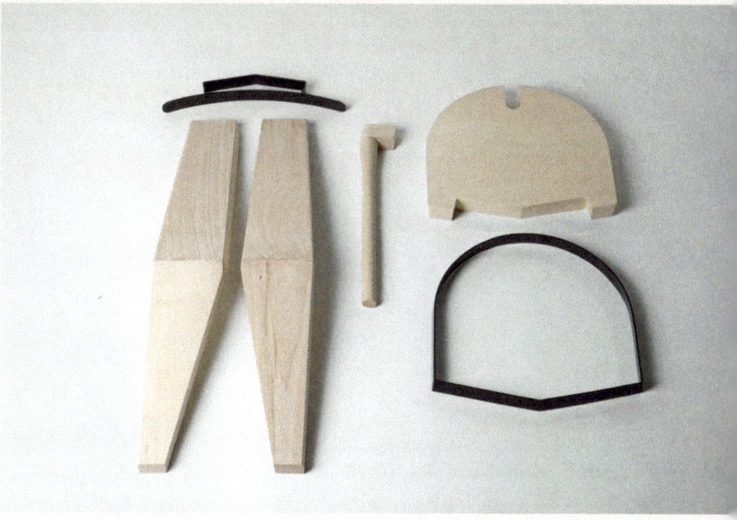

Blanc's easy-to-assemble chair can be described as a DIY kit. He based his design on a method for making barrels.
Photos courtesy of ÉCAL

Clamped Stools
by Daniel Glazman
Bezalel Academy of Arts and Design, Israel
be.net/danielglazman

'In Israel, the term "Israeli work" often refers to unprofessional working methods. Observing carpenters, welders, locksmiths and other craftspeople, I discovered that they all improvise, often making tools from materials close at hand when they need something for a specific job. I wanted to employ this kind of improvisation in my project.'

For his first model, Glazman used a clamp to hold two boards together. In the final design, the clamp that keeps the entire construction together is integrated into one leg of the stool.
Photos Oded Antman

Shape Shifters
Engaging, interactive and adaptable objects

The Oturakast is flexible. Its components, which serve as both drawers and stools, come in different sizes and colours; they can be stacked as desired.

Oturakast

by Rianne Koens
Design Academy Eindhoven
The Netherlands
riannekoens.com

'Inspired by the warm hospitality of my Turkish in-laws, I conceived the Oturakast. The Turkish word for 'sit' is *otur*, and the word for 'stool' is *oturak*. This chest of drawers is intended for a Western interior that may not be furnished for receiving guests at short notice. It consists of a stack of separate storage components with legs that fold out, turning drawers into stools. When visitors leave, you fold up the legs, stack the stools-cum-drawers and have a complete cabinet again.'

Bundle can be used as a bench or a stool. It features a removable component, which can be rolled up, that is made from wooden dowels covered in merino felt or Waterborn (Kvadrat).

Bundle

by Catherine Aitken
Royal College of Art, UK
catherinelouiseaitken.co.uk

'Bundle is loosely inspired by actions of organization: stacking, rolling and bundling. I wanted to make a collection of furniture that encourages touch – that is inviting. I like the idea of repetition as a simple way to develop a three-dimensional product. As a textile designer, I am interested in exploring materials Bundle consists of two elements – one hard, one soft – which are equally dependent on each other.'

Not What It Seems
Familiar things seen in a new light

Isometric Mirrors
by Germans Ermičs
Design Academy Eindhoven
The Netherlands
germansermics.com

'Being very interested in optical illusions, I wanted to make a simple interior object with an unexpected element. We look into the mirror to get a sense of reality. In the reflection, we expect to see the world as it is, nothing more. What happens when a tweaked reality gazes back at us, thus altering our perception of what is real?'

A curved strip of wood framing Ermičs' oval mirrors makes the objects look like holes in the wall. Several mirrors next to one another intensify the confusion, making parts of the wall appear to shift and tilt.

Meshmatics

by Rick Tegelaar
ArtEZ, the Netherlands
ricktegelaar.nl

'The idea for Meshmatics emerged during a project for which we were asked to look at everyday life in a new way. I discovered a highly controlled method of making objects out of chicken wire. By cutting chicken wire from a roll at a 45-degree angle, I made square holes into diamond-shaped openings and used the material to create clean, aesthetically pleasing forms. Looking at something in a slightly different way can lead to a maximum result.'

With an inverted press of his own design, which relies on 'pull' rather than 'push', Tegelaar shapes chicken wire into aesthetic lampshades that he wraps in wet bamboo paper.

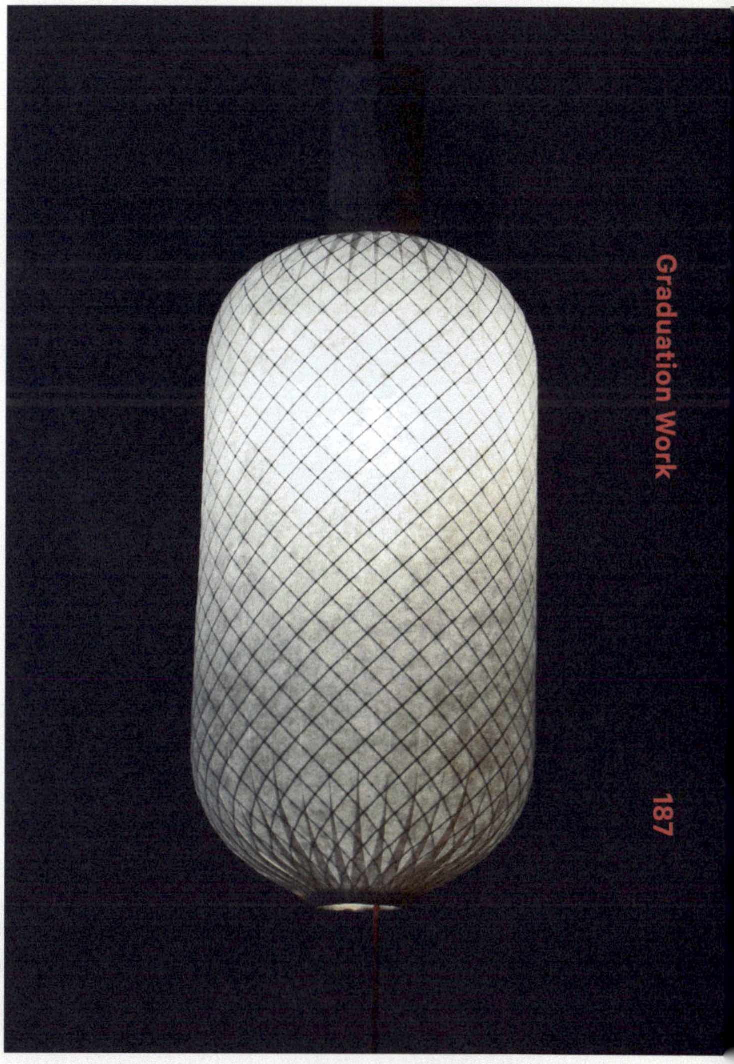

Conceptual Tabletops
Everyday items shaped by shadow and use

For a tableware collection, Wassink designed new forms, which she made from well-considered materials that emphasize the action for which each object is intended.

Daily Movements

by Wendy Wassink
ArtEZ, the Netherlands
wendywassink.nl

'My collection is about the beauty of simple actions. To focus all attention on the act of pouring, I avoided every form of decoration. The materials reinforce the sensory experience of the action involved. I used aluminium for the sugar pot, for example, to amplify the sound of scooping sugar from the container. My products turn everyday situations into refined rituals.'

Trace of Shadow

by Kijtanes Kajornrattanadech
Central Saint Martins, UK
kijtanes.com

'Shadow can prevent objects from appearing flat or two-dimensional. It allows our eyes to see the third dimension. Shadow is what makes everything on this planet complete. An object without a shadow simply doesn't exist. I wanted to design a collection that makes shadow a tangible part of daily life, an experience that also has a useful function.'

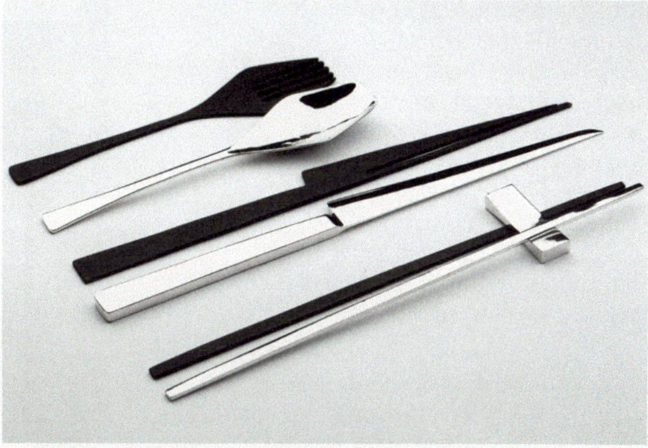

Kajornrattanadech provides cups, bowls and cutlery with shadows that can be used as placemats or coasters.

Form Follows Method
Innovative techniques produce one-offs

Gravity Stool

Jólan van der Wiel
Gerrit Rietveld Academy
The Netherlands
jolanvanderwiel.com

'Everything is subject to the influence of gravity, which strongly affects shape. I set out to manipulate this natural phenomenon using its own power: magnetism. I made my first forms by experimenting with magnets and materials mixed with powdered iron. Because I wanted the result to be a functional object, I also developed a machine that simplifies the production of a small series of stools.'

Opposing fields of two magnets, along with gravity, turn ferriferous material into a stool whose shape is reminiscent of tree bark, lava or other organic forms.
Photos Jac van der Wiel

Blast Chairs by Explosion

Guy Mishaly
Bezalel Academy of Arts and Design, Israel
guymishaly.com

'Creating something positive out of destruction has always fascinated me. Nature does it in several ways – with fire, for example – and humans use implosion and explosion. I did research on the behaviour of explosives and their influence on materials. It was a challenge to find a way to control the energy and to make an entire object by pressing a button.'

Each Blast stool starts out as a geometric shape made of sheet metal that is webbed with explosive material. The explosion creates legs and makes each object unique.
Photos Oded Antman

Shaping the Future

The future of design seems to belong to 3D printing, but just how fast is the technology developing?

Words **Jeroen Junte**

The RepRap – a rudimentary 3D printer capable of producing all the components needed to build a 3D printer – is available on the internet for as little as US$500.
Photo courtesy of Adrian Bowyer

The paperclip is one of the world's oldest industrial designs. Since the invention of this ingenious device in 1867, the world has seen the emergence of new materials such as plastic – not to mention technologies like advanced computer design. Despite such giant leaps in progress, however, billions of people continue to use metal paperclips that look like the one first produced nearly 145 years ago. But change is in the air. Earlier this year, Belgian 3D-printing service i.materialise posted a design for a 'better paperclip' on thingiverse.com. A visitor to the site can download the design file – at no charge – and make the nifty figure-eight clip by simply pressing a button on his personal 3D printer.

A new paperclip – not exactly the first thing that pops to mind when a revolution in design and production is mentioned. Then, too, the Belgian firm's Infinite Clip isn't the first variation on the bent-wire original to hit the market, and every alternative has to compete with the clever 19th-century design conceived by American Samuel Fay. The new model by i.materialise could turn out to be a success story, though, since it doesn't require the development of an expensive, complicated manufacturing and distribution system. Today's *prosumer* – part producer, part consumer – buys the product directly from the designer.

So, yes, a 'printed' paperclip does herald a revolution in design and production, says Kevin Nichols, consumer service manager at Shapeways, a New York company spawned by Philips Electronics. 'What's revolutionary is that 3D printing negates mass-production. Thanks to the 3D printer, the cost price of a product is always the same, whether you make 10,000 units or only one. Products no longer have to be manufactured in bulk and transported across the globe. They're produced locally – in small batches or as one-offs – using local materials. The saving in costs is considerable.' Moreover, 3D printing follows the principle of additive manufacturing (in which a 3D model supplies data for the creation of an object made from material that is usually applied in many wafer-thin layers) rather than that of subtractive manufacturing (the traditional method, which involves reduction rather than augmentation). 'The precise amount of material needed is used, and not a bit more.'

Nonetheless, 3D-printing is not always cost-effective. Compare, for example, the cost of the material used to print a product – which can easily reach €60 a kg – with the €2-a-kg cost of plastic used for rotomoulding. In some cases, mass-production is also more efficient. On the other hand, says Nichols, 3D-printed products are completed in one go. 'Series production often means making moulds, or even setting up a special production line before you can get started.' The production of items that have to adapt to circumstances such as weather can also benefit from 3D printing. 'A minute modification in the design drawing is often all that's needed when you want an adapted version of an existing product,' he says. 'It's quick and easy.' A final advantage of printing is the realization of virtually impossible forms and

Laminated Object Manufacturing (LOM)

This is the oldest method of digital production. The patent was filed in 1985. Layers of adhesive-coated paper, plastic or metal are glued together, and shapes are cut from the resulting sheet material with a knife or laser cutter. Currently, the technology is used only for the creation of complex prototypes and scale models that demand a great deal of handwork and modification.

History in Print

The first 3D printer was developed in the mid-1980s by an American who based his invention on a machine that used cartridges to apply fast-drying paint. By substituting fast-drying resin for paint, he was able to print simple objects. In the '90s, the aerospace and automotive industries, along with other advanced organizations, continued to develop the technology, which has been used primarily to make complex prototypes, giving rise to the term 'rapid prototyping'.

constructions. 'Even the most advanced factory machines can't offer the design freedom you get with an average 3D printer.'

Traditional manufacturers can also incorporate the benefits of the 3D-printer into their business plans. One way would be to post the specifications of a product's more vulnerable components on the company website. When a component needs to be replaced, the consumer can download the relevant design file and print out the part in question. By raising the initial price of the product to cover this service, the manufacturer can eliminate the intensive system of distributing and selling separate components.

The real 3D-printing revolution, says Nichols, lies in the unprecedented freedom of choice afforded the consumer. His company is already offering over 10,000 products, which can be adapted to the consumer's individual wishes. You can also have your self-designed products fabricated by Shapeways. 'At the moment we supply products in any of 12 materials, ranging from stainless steel and plastic to the more recently added ceramic. Theoretically, anything that sticks together is suitable for 3D printing. It's also possible to print objects in different colours. It won't be long before people are designing and making products at home in all shapes and sizes and in every conceivable material and colour.'

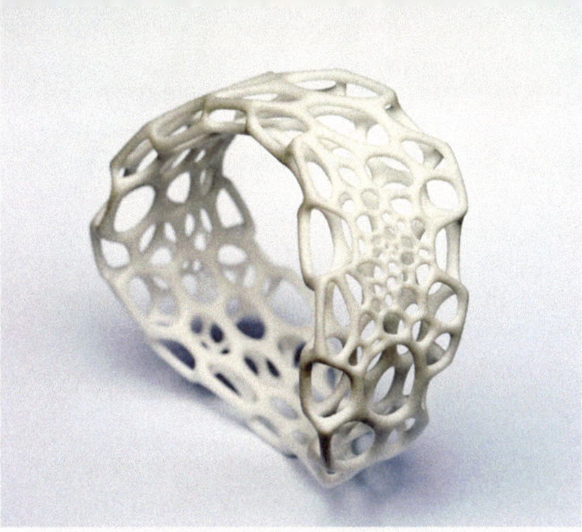

Nervous System's Subdivision Bracelet is 3D printed in polyamide.
Photo courtesy of Shapeways

An important stimulus for large-scale home production is the RepRap, which stands for 'replicating rapid prototyper'. The RepRap is a rudimentary 3D printer that is capable of producing all the components you need to build a 3D printer. These cloning machines are available on the internet for as little as US$500, a price that makes them accessible to a wide range of consumers, but they are slower and less precise than professional printers. On the brighter side, RepRaps are an eco-friendly step towards sustainable production. Adrian Bowyer, a professor at the University of Bath and the man who designed RepRap, has also developed a recyclable 3D-printing material. An obsolete product is pulverized and the resulting powder used to print a new object. Taking the concept a step further, Markus Kayser, a student at the Royal College of Art in London, came up with SolarSinter, a 3D printer that uses solar energy to convert desert sand into objects or parts made of glass. Think of the unrivalled opportunities that this machine, which costs only a few hundred dollars and generates its own energy, can furnish African entrepreneurs.

In view of the speed at which such innovations are appearing, surely it's only a matter of time ...

Part of Philips' food-design probe, this conceptual food printer combines various edible elements, which it makes into a desired shape and consistency.
Photo courtesy of Philips

The 3D-printing revolution means freedom of choice for the consumer

Stereolithography

Another early technology is stereolithography, in which a laser beam cures a light-sensitive liquid polymer, layer by layer, gradually building up an object. The process requires a supporting platform, which sinks slowly into a vat of liquid polymer. As the platform is immersed, a specific UV laser wavelength creates and solidifies each layer of the object.

... before the less expensive models can do the job as well as today's commercial 3D printers. Scientists at Cornell University in New York have already used 3D food printers to 'prepare' edible creations with ingredients like flour, herbs and natural thickeners, such as potato starch. Rapid developments are taking place in the medical sector as well. Earlier this year, the first heart-transplant operation was reportedly carried out using a 3D-printed artificial heart. The ultimate achievement would entail the printing of living cells. In one potential scenario, healthy skin cells harvested from a person with serious wounds or burns are cloned and then applied to the patient with a kind of jet printer, layer by layer, until the injured areas are protected by healthy skin.

Jim Scanlan, professor of aerospace design at the University of Southampton, is the first person to use a 3D printer to make a model aeroplane that flies.
Photo courtesy of Jim Scanlan

We still have a way to go, however. Most 3D printers are expensive: prices, which don't include materials, vary from €1500 for a very simple personal printer to €15,000 for a basic industrial model. You need to know enough about computers to work with the required design software, and you need to be aware of the machine's limitations. It uses only one material to make one product at a time. Natural materials like wood and rubber are not yet suitable for 3D printers. Not for nothing do we find ready-made 3D-printed items online, and then primarily on iTunes-like websites such as shapeways.com, ponoko.com and thingiverse.com: in essence, a handful of virtual mail-order companies with a vast selection of merchandise. At present, none of the products offered is much larger than an average Samsonite suitcase. Shapeways, for example, has no metal products that exceed 1 m, and the firm's largest glass product is a mere 8 cm.

'Anything that sticks together is suitable for 3D printing'

The 3D printer is introducing new legal problems as well. For example, thingiverse.com, which offers free downloads, recently removed (for the first time) a design from its site owing to copyright infringement. This seems like a rearguard action, though, since once a design is on the internet, any attempt to prevent illegal copying is no more than a hopeless act of desperation. 'Designers who make downloadable designs need to consider alternative business models,' is the response of Joris Laarman, who's looking for new ways to manufacture and distribute his high-profile Bone Chair (see *Frame* 54, pp. 158-160). 'When a design's been downloaded and reproduced over and over, it's time to think about earning money with signed limited editions, for instance. Another source of income might be a manufacturer who steps in and starts producing a design that's being downloaded by a significant number of people – because I don't see masses of people retreating to their garages and fabricating entire interiors. Compare it to paper printouts. You print a simple A4-format page at home, but when you want a full-colour, bound book you go to a professional printer.'

Selective Laser Sintering (SLS)

A popular technology, SLS employs a CO2 laser to create an object layer by layer. The laser scans 3D digital cross sections on the surface of a powder bed, heating (almost to the melting point) the tiny particles of powder until they fuse together. As successive layers of powder are added and heated, one at a time, an object is created. The technology produces very strong objects and is suitable for a wide range of materials, but it does not allow for smooth surfaces and highly precise shapes.

Capable of using solar energy to convert desert sand into objects made of glass, Markus Kayser's SolarSinter is seen here in the Sahara Desert. The process used to print a square glass tile is shown below.
Photos Amos Field Reid

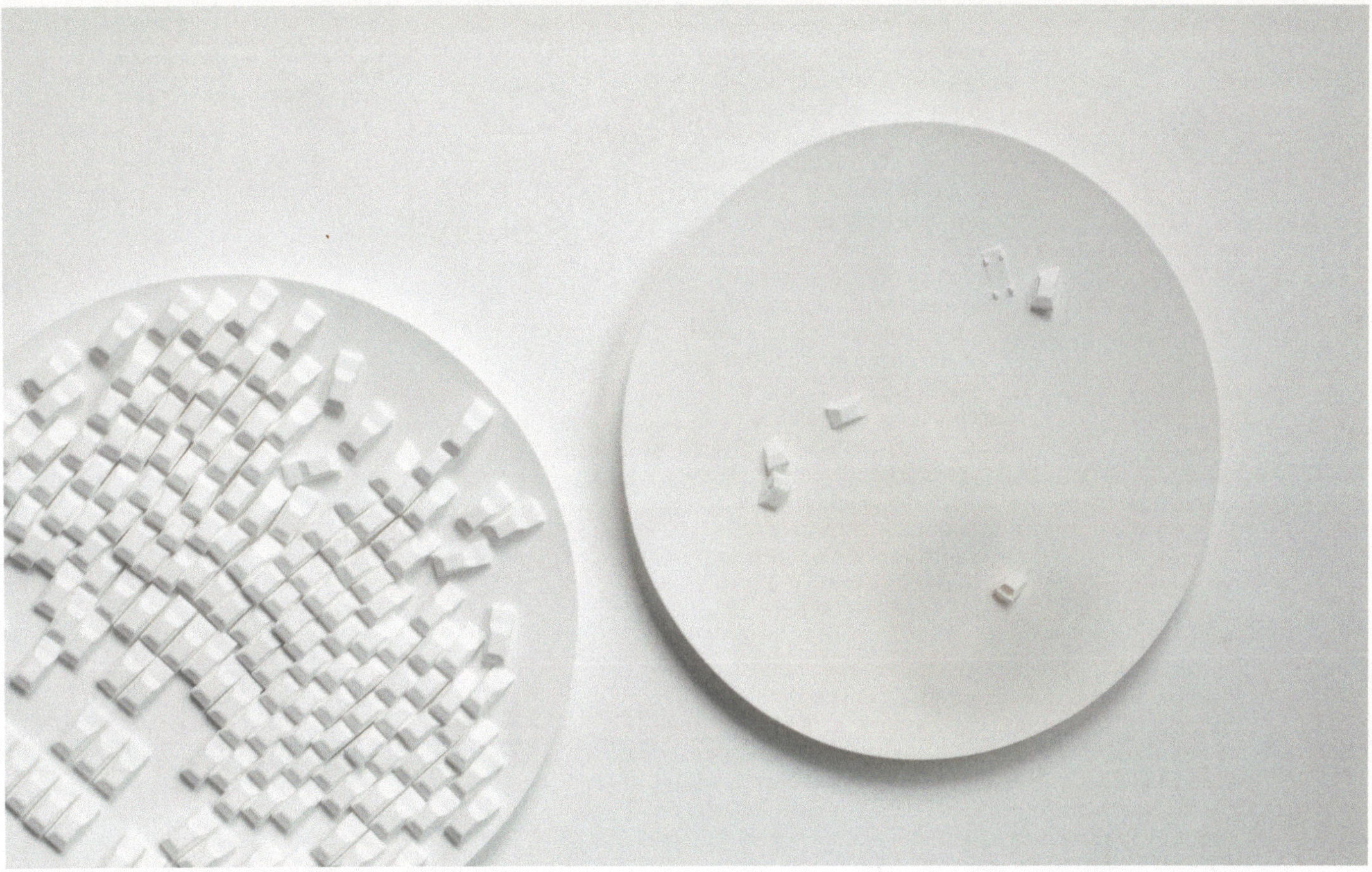

Reflecting the sea of online content available for 3D printing, Maya Ben David's memorial plate fossilizes a photograph of floating cars to create a symbol of the recent tsunami in Japan.

Laarman collaborated with Dutch design label Droog to develop make-me.com, an online platform that was presented at the 2011 Salone del Mobile. Make-me.com couples manual production with digital production involving 3D printers. 'Consumers can look for a local workshop where they can make the design they downloaded,' says Droog project manager Mariëlle Janmaat. 'If it's a table, for example, they can have the legs printed and work with a carpenter to make a wooden tabletop.' Thanks to make-me.com's user-friendly software, the digital-design process is accessible to all. 'With this program, even a computer noob can create a 3D form from a 2D grid. The computer-animated shape is converted instantly into a drawing that is recognized by digital machines. The program helps someone equipped with nothing more than a computer mouse to design his own desk,' says Janmaat.

Joris Laarman is searching for new ways to manufacture and distribute his high-profile Bone Chair.
Photo Bas Helbers

A system that revolves totally around the 'consumer as producer' was conceived by Belgian designer Thomas Lommee, whose Open Structures (OS) is a modular grid that invites laypeople and professionals to design standard products. 'It makes product design easier. Consumers can immediately exchange ideas and information that emerge during the design or production process, because everybody's using the same system. It's comparable to Wikipedia, whose users refine and update articles all the time,' says Lommee. A vital aspect of Open Structures is its matter-of-fact approach to recycling. 'When a product is broken, its individual components can still be used.'

Currently, Lommee's platform is limited to a website: openstructures.net. Later this year in Brussels, he will open the first physical meeting place for users. 'The project is still in development,' he says. The key question is: what economic system works best for this type of production? 'Should we open an online shop and sell OS designs? Or would it be better to come up with an alternative system? The lack of an earnings model for users is sure to stifle innovation.' He's not plagued by doubt, though. 'The 3D printer is here to stay. No one knows what the future will bring. Two hundred years ago, who could have predicted the impact of the steam engine on society?' _

Inkjet Technology

Inkjet technology is at the heart of most commercial 3D printers and RepRaps. An inkjet using a bonding agent draws an object in a layer of powder (plaster of Paris, resin or even metal), which subsides to allow the addition of a new layer of powder. The process is repeated until all layers have been printed. An alternative to the use of a bonding agent is to fuse the layers of powder together with a thermal laser photopolymer lamp, which offers the designer more freedom. Earlier this year a student at the Massachusetts Institute of Technology (MIT) in Boston printed – in one go – a complete grandfather clock with dozens of components. He added a counterweight, and the clock started ticking.

Colani demonstrates with great aplomb how to use his Meditation chair (1973): 'Do this every day; you'll never have back problems.' When asked whether he uses the chair daily, he replies, 'I don't need to.'

Captain Colani

In the fourth in a series of talks with designers who've earned their spurs, Luigi Colani discusses the state of design worldwide in a marathon performance.

Words **Katya Tylevich**
Photos **Alexei Tylevich**

Sporting his signature white attire and puffing on a cigar, Professor Luigi Colani orders a round of cappuccinos for us, which grow cold as the conversation grows more heated. That's day one of our 'blah-blah-blah', as Colani calls it. We sit in the large outdoor patio of the hotel where Colani is staying, some 25 minutes northwest of Milan's city centre and some 500 m from Colani's Milanese studio. I feel as if I'm in a performance-art piece: Colani and Tylevich in a competition of endurance – who will break from this marathon conversation first? 'I could talk for many more hours,' Colani tells me. 'You'll be tired before I am.'

Around us, the entrance patio is lined with Colani-designed automobiles: biomorphic creatures that look fast even though they're standing still; they make the cabbie who drops us off at the hotel whistle in amazement. Cabbie should get a load of Colani's aircraft designs and prototypes of flying boats, or his loudspeakers that nod to contours of the inner ear, or his ergonomic house-painting tools that yield to the shape of the human hand. He should see Bio-City, Colani's urban concept in the form of a human body. *Mamma mia*! – to quote Colani, who claims the two-word exclamation is the extent of his Italian vocabulary. Born in Berlin in 1928, he has lived and worked in numerous corners of the world, most recently in China, and has an opinion about the state of design in all of them.

Day two: Colani picks us up in a two-door Jaguar and rockets to his studio, where more coffee grows cold as Colani shows me his architectural renderings, the book ('to end all books about design') he's working on, and his sketches for a car ('to end all motor cars'). Here, we are surrounded by Colani chairs; Colani cups, saucers and teapots; 20 statues of naked Olympic athletes, which Colani designed for the Olympics in Beijing; chairs meant to ply the human figure into a meditative state; and, most importantly, Colani's enormous personality. It's no wonder the man's been made into an action figure.

You've been working in China for the past several years. I didn't expect to find you in Milan.

I never wanted to come here. Never. Why should I – Colani – come to Italy? They have good designers here already! But they called like mad for Colani. My father is from the Italian part of Switzerland, and I have an Italian name. They want Italian-sounding names here. [Laughs.] I don't speak a word of Italian. This guy – a great Colani fan – had visited me many times. We spoke about a sort of hub for this design-minded city. I gradually made the decision to come and stay here. And I like it. It is a wonderful country, Italy. Of course, I still have to do business in China. I spend maybe half the year there, and the rest in Moscow, Milano, South America.

While you were working in China, many of the interviews you gave seemed quite negative about design in Europe and the United States. You found it conservative, compared with what was happening in China.

I'm of the generation that was very fond of American design in the '50s and '60s. It was the absolute top of the world. Nobody could even think of being half as good as American designers. And those dream cars that came out of their studios! But things fluctuate: what goes up goes down. Even the Japanese, who were very good when I was working with them 20 years ago, have gone blub, blub, blub, down. They have one car recall after another; they have trouble all over the place. *Mamma mia*!

But, yes, I've been very negative about recent American design. America needs a lot of help. All they're doing at the moment is repairing the bad things they've done. The auto-industry bosses are rotten conservatives. Nothing's coming from General Motors. Nothing's coming from Ford. ...

'Things fluctuate: what goes up goes down'

A collection of Colani's seating designs includes the infamous Garden Chair, designed in 1967 (foreground).

... Nothing's coming from Chrysler. And so on. It's an enormous pity.

Is there any way to speak about design in a global sense? Can you pinpoint one or more common themes, or is the subject of design geographically fragmented?
That's a very complicated question. Today, I see no place in the world where design is at home. Italy is down. Germany was never anything to begin with: Germans are good technicians, but not good designers – and I'll tell you why later. The Scandinavian countries have very good designers, but they are too tranquil. Things are shifting now in terms of money as well. Asia is coming on strong, sometimes too strong. Money, money, money, money, money. Asians were hungry. They had nothing at all. Now they have something, and they want more of it.

You're painting a very grim picture.
It's not grim. We haven't even started talking yet. Design is shifting in the underground. There is no country in the world that can call itself number one – not Italy, not any place. Design is nowhere today. Nowhere.
Having said that, I admit that design is wherever an individual has the guts to step away from the crowd and say: I can do it better. And there are many, many young people – unknown designers – around the world doing just that. They are very good, very promising, yet having their ideas killed by teachers and professors, of course. Terrific young people with super ideas: in Albania, in Greece, in Africa. The world is utterly positive. Is that clear? There are some dirty forces behind the curtain doing evil things, but the world is utterly positive. Next question.

[Colani looks at the Canon 5D camera my brother, Alexei, is using to take photos of him.] What type of camera is that? Canon? That's a Colani design from 25 years ago. Normally, a designer designs for the present. I design things for tomorrow that nobody wants today. They want them 25 years later. Actually, I do design for today. It's the CEOs who don't accept the ideas when they first see them. They are too anxious and too stupid. So I wait. I am like a woman. I have patience. Endless patience.

At the start of his career, Colani provided illustrations for automobile magazines.

It sounds remarkably frustrating.
Do I look frustrated? I am very happy. Guys like me would have been burned at the stake in previous ages. They would have killed me, because I don't think like normal people. Drink your coffee – if you can, that is, out of *that* cup. Look at the stupid thing. It's a miracle you can put your finger through the handle. You have to be careful not to let it slip. Now if you were drinking out of a Colani cup, that would never happen.
See, a good designer has to consider comfort. The bed in which I lie, the seat on which I sit, the shoes or trousers I wear – all have to be comfortable. When I notice that the need for comfort is not satisfied, the brain starts

'The job of a designer is a very political one'

The entrance of the ATAhotel Expo Fiera is festooned with Colani cars.

Fitted with a BMW engine, the Small Hovercraft (1998, mock-up) – a two- to four-seater AVC (air-cushion vehicle) – is designed to travel at speeds of up to 150 km/h.

working. This is design, and nothing more. I am still doing the same things I did 40 or 50 years ago. I haven't changed, because I know what is good for human use.

Maybe you haven't changed in 50 years, but surely the environment in which you work has changed.

Truck based on a DAF chassis. In *Colani: The Complete Oeuvre: The Book Accompanying the Exhibition*, the author questions why Colani's ideas, which he propagated for 30 years, were never adopted by the automobile industry.

No. Manufacturers are as conservative as they were when I started: 'our clientele doesn't want this', or 'this is too advanced', or 'make it a bit different'. That's when I say, no thank you. Bye, bye. I feel lucky that I make enough money to be able to pay for the things I create. I earned this money so that I could fulfil my dreams. And if people reject what I design, I don't care. They will discover it in time.

Do you work for yourself?
Not at all. I work for the people. My language is understood in the real world, even if it is not understood by CEOs. Look, I work alongside my employees. I talk to them. I come from a simple family of normal, loving parents, nice brothers and sisters. Lots of laughter. Not too much money, but very happy. I haven't changed. I was lucky to be brought up in a clear-cut and sober way. I don't depend on anybody. Today, only men like me can tell the truth. Others can't, because their bosses will immediately sack them.

On the public level, though – apart from CEOs – has public understanding of design changed?
Yes. Enormously. People are critical. They know how badly they are treated by those at the top. Humans today are victim to a thin layer of rich people and the government, so the job of a designer is a very political one. Think about what happens if I give a country a super design: I am automatically killing companies in other countries with my good design. Imagine that one company builds my truck, which consumes 40 per cent less fuel. Other companies wouldn't be able to sell even one car of a different design. I have to be a very political thinker.

Do you still have a studio in Berlin?
No. I've left Germany altogether. Finished. And I'll tell you why. Because Germany is a dirty dictatorship of minimalism that has falsified the original Bauhaus testament drawn up by Gropius, Wassily Kandinsky, and Mies van der Rohe.

After World War II, German designers skipped the pyramid, skipped the circle and put colour away. Bauhaus today is steel, glass, concrete, wood and square. This represents my struggle. I began as a sculptor, and art is integral to my work. But Germans fight against art and against any soft, humanizing touch in design, so I'm their biggest, baddest enemy. I attack Bauhaus: here in Milano, in Russia and in South America. We are working as a neo-Bauhaus. ...

A model aeroplane in Colani's studio. The designer's father – whom Colani describes as 'a super-technician, super-artist, sculptor and painter' – greatly influenced his career.

'I design things for tomorrow that nobody wants today'

... Germany threw me out. I'm nothing in Germany, nothing at all, because I told them they are wrong. Those dirty professors fight Colani whenever they can. Look at the bathtubs of today, and the toilets and the bidets and the washbasins. [Sketches squares on a napkin.] I could kill those designers. Inhuman things. Impossible.

The world is round; our blue planet is round. Why work against it? Nature is so wonderful and so much older than this thing we call 'humanity'. We are one of the youngest specimens on the planet, yet we have done the worst things to it. Look at Fukushima, eh? Look at Chernobyl.

Are you disappointed in humans?
Not in the simple ones, the common people. I love them. But the ones up top – they didn't get there through knowledge. They got there by sticking their elbows out and pushing others out of the way.

When we spoke earlier, you told me your father was a stage designer for film. Do you think he influenced you in any way?
Oh, enormously. He was much better than I am. He was enormous. A super-technician, a super-artist, sculptor and painter. He was sensational. I learned so much from him. I'm the only kid in the world that ran straight home from school. I didn't want to play. I ran home because my father was there, working on small models of stages.

What kinds of films did he work on?
Many old famous German films of the '30s, '40s and '50s. The last film he made was with Leni Riefenstahl, *Tiefland*, a famous opera. He made all the designs for the original version of *Titanic*. We still have a box of cigars from that film – made out of paper. Beautiful! As a kid, I got to be in some of the films. I remember having to eat a big slice of bread with marmalade on it. I always looked at the camera. I can still hear the stage whispers. *Don't look at the camera!*

So your first profession was actor.
I was an actor – a small George Clooney!

Was that when you started wanting to create things?
No, I started working very early with modelling clay. At my house, we had all the things a graphic designer needs. And I was always inclined to see things in a natural way. When I was a child, I spent lots of time at the zoo, looking at lions, birds, insects – anything that moved. When I saw seals and sharks underwater – *mamma mia*! – those incredible shapes, especially compared with our stupid shapes. [Laughs.] Unbeatable. You can't beat nature. _

Frustrated with 'stupid' cups and saucers, Colani designed his own. He also developed similarly eccentric egg cups (right).

‘I am like a woman. I have patience. Endless patience’

One of 20 statues of nude Olympians that Colani designed for the Beijing 2008 Olympic Games.

Colani talks shop in his showroom-esque studio in Milan.

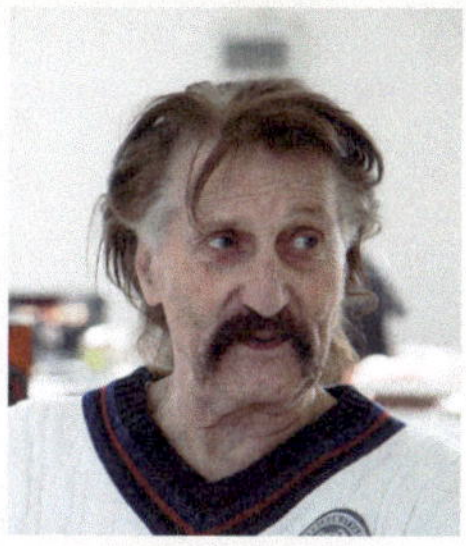

Luigi Colani

1928 Born in Berlin
1946 Studies sculpture at the Akademie der Künste Berlin
1948 Studies aerodynamics at the Sorbonne in Paris
1954 Starts designing for Fiat
1957 Designs Colani Alfa sports car
1959 Designs BMW 700 sports car
1965 Designs furniture for Asko, Fritz Hanzen, Cor, Kusch+Co
1973 Establishes Colani Design Center Japan
1978 Presents revolutionary truck, aircraft, car and ship studies
1982 Relocates to Japan
1983 Professor in Tokyo
1986 Designs Canon T-90; founds Colani Design Bern, Switzerland
1988 Opens offices in Toulouse and Bremen; professor h.c. at Hochschule für Gestaltung, Bremen
1989 Establishes Colani Trading AG in Zürich
1991 Sets world record with Colani Ferrari at Bonneville Speedway in Utah
1995 Opens new head office of Colani's design works in Cologne; is awarded professorship at Tongji University, Shanghai
1996 Presents Bio-City, an architecture concept for Shanghai
1997 Designs new piano for Schimmel
1998 Starts bank-terminal design project
2001 Designs new microscope and camera at Colani Shanghai office
2002 Spitzer-Silo presents new Colani truck at IAA-Hannover, Germany
2003 Designs TT 62 plane for HPA
2006 Completes Colani Supertruck
2008 Opens design studio in Beihai, China
2010 Opens studio in Milan, Italy
2011 Works from studios in China, Italy, Russia and South America

Step on It

Swiss art duo Lang/Baumann conjures up a surreal series of staircases to nowhere.

Words **Jane Szita**
Photos **courtesy of Lang/Baumann**

The vertigo-inducing *Beautiful Steps #2*, Bienne, Switzerland, 2009.

'We love their dreamlike quality'

Keeping viewers in suspense: the seemingly weightless (but actually very heavy) *Beautiful Steps #3*, Le Confort Moderne, Poitiers, France, 2009.

Artists Sabina Lang (1972, Bern) and Daniel Baumann (1967, San Francisco) have been producing work together as Lang/Baumann or L/B since the early 1990s. Inspired by both pop art and Bauhaus, Lang/Baumann's work includes installations, sculptures, architectural interventions and 'relational strategies'. The artists' series of staircase installations perversely places a functional architectural element in an unexpected, nonfunctional context.

What inspired you to work with stairs?
Sabina Lang (SL): The fact that they form an architectural element that is immediately familiar to the viewer. This means people are willing to take the first step in approaching the installation. Only when they take a second step – and realize that this isn't like a normal staircase – do their questions come up.

Where and when did you do the first of these pieces?
SL: The first one following this logic was the *Beautiful Steps #2* installation for the Swiss Sculpture Exhibition in Bienne in 2009.

How many staircases have you done now?
Daniel Baumann (DB): We've done six in total. One [*Beautiful Steps #3*] was presented twice in totally different spaces: once at Le Confort Moderne, an industrial space, and once at Trautenfels, a baroque castle. Our seventh staircase is planned for 2012 in Lyon.

Which one was the most difficult?
DB: *Beautiful Steps #5* was probably the most complicated. The stairs had to wrap around an old tower, high above the ground. It wasn't possible to use a crane, and the construction was as heavy as hell.

Where would you most like to put your next staircase?
SL: In a natural context – perhaps a forest or a garden would be interesting.

Do the stair pieces convey a message?
DB: It depends on the individual situation. Often, it's about imagination – visualizing how it would be to use these stairs suspended in space and to enjoy the view from a place far up on a building's façade. A whole story emerges. We also like the dreamlike quality that comes from suspending a massive, heavy piece in the air like this.

How do people react to the staircases?
With surprise, confusion, admiration – sometimes irritation.

How do these installations relate to the rest of your work?
It's always about notions of perception and public space, but we constantly try to expand our range, our language and the tools we use.

langbaumann.com

Beautiful Steps #5, Schloss Trautenfels, Styria, Austria, 2010. Outside the windows, the staircase wraps around a castle tower, high above the ground.

The Great Unknown

Rather than walking a fine line between design and art, Ignotus Nomen unites both disciplines within an unusually honest collection.

Words **Femke de Wild**
Photos **courtesy of Galerie Kreo**

It's alleged that Pierre Charpin's latest collection for Galerie Kreo does have a name, but it's completely unknown, even to the maker. Meanwhile his new series of eight pieces – bench, cabinet, bookshelf, coffee table, console, desk, lamp and vase – remains Ignotus Nomen. Each item contains two parts: a minimalist interior product made of glass, wood or Krion (a composite, solid-surface material) and a sculptural resin object painted black or white. Galerie Kreo introduced the pieces in June 2011 at Design Miami Basel, but the greater public got its first glimpse of the collection several months later, when it appeared at the gallery in Paris.

Educated as an artist, Charpin discovered early on that his real interest lay in the creation of furniture and objects. Although composed not entirely of practical pieces, his *oeuvre* reveals a marked emphasis on functionality. In addition to austere forms that straddle the boundary between art and design, Charpin is known most widely for his use of colour. Long before colour in the interior began its most recent advance, Charpin had employed subtle shades and even bold contrasts in his work.

Never before were Charpin's two interests represented as clearly as they are in his designs for the Ignotus Nomen collection. These pieces do not tread a fine line between art and design but express the qualities of both – and they do it well. Tables, storage units, lamp, bench and vase: all are genuinely functional products whose cleanly drawn contours radiate a look of simplicity befitting any contemporary interior. Reduced to the bare minimum, Charpin's sculptural accompaniments are reminiscent of early 20th-century work by the likes of Constantin Brancusi. The polished sheen and abstracted autonomy of these objects make no direct reference to anything, inviting observers to come up with personal interpretations. Charpin has even avoided conspicuous colour here, limiting himself to contrasts that rely on white, black and natural wood tones.

Since each functional object coexists with an enigmatic sculpture, potential descriptions are rife. The smooth black 'rock' at one end of the bench can be used as an armrest, but the sculpture also transforms the bench into a pedestal worthy of a museum exhibition. Art and design are exemplified in separate objects, but these objects interact to such a degree that we invariably question the boundary between disciplines. This quandary is what makes Ignotus Nomen one of the more honest examples of design art to have emerged in recent years. _

Ignotus Nomen

Design Pierre Charpin (pierrecharpin.com)
Materials Honeycomb panel, resin, Krion, hand-blown opal glass, chestnut, paint
Description Series of 8 objects
Edition Limited edition of 8 pieces + 2 AP + 2 prototypes of each object
Gallery Galerie Kreo (galeriekreo.fr)

Of all Charpin's sculptural objects in the series, the one he designed for the lamp merges with its functional partner to create the strongest entity.

One end of the bench is occupied by a black sculpture that forms a basis for all the objects that appear in the Ignotus Nomen collection.

Supporting a black sculpture, a tall white cabinet bears a striking resemblance to the type of pedestal used to display art in a museum.

Never before were Charpin's two interests so clearly represented

Instead of an impressive volume of art or architecture, a gleaming white object takes pride of place on the coffee table.

Discount Days

Guaranteed delivery before 24 December

From 15 to 30 November, Frame Publishers is offering 30% off selected books and magazines.

Purchase titles like *Grand Stand 3*, *Material World 3* and recent release *Colour Hunting*, plus issues of *Frame*, *Mark* and *Elephant*, all for bargain prices.

Buy online at frameweb.com/sale

FRAME

Making It

Can't afford a designer sofa? A new book explains how to make your own Julia Lohmann, Rich Brilliant Willing or Peter Marigold creation.

Words **Jane Szita**

There are some pretty well-known names among the contributors to *DIY Furniture*. Was it hard to get them to release their work for free?
Chris Stuart: Yes and no. Originally, I wanted to include more budding designers. But as it turned out, the bigger names saw the value in the idea immediately, while many of the up-and-comers didn't want to contribute their designs for free.

Who owns the copyrights of the designs in the book?
The designers do – they've just shared the instructions for making the pieces. Legally, the designs can be made for personal use only, not for resale.

How much potential does this concept have?
Plenty. I see a trend towards DIY, because of the economy. People are becoming more resourceful and are willing to do more to save money. People are simplifying their lives. They are choosing more carefully and surrounding themselves with things that resonate with them more, or just function better.

You're an artist and designer yourself. Why do a book?
The idea came after the firm I worked for closed its doors as a result of the downturn in the economy.

How did you arrive at this concept?
I can't take total credit. I originally pitched it as a DIY lighting book, but the publisher thought it would be better to include other home furnishings. They were right. The book has far more variety this way.

Why make your own furniture, anyway?
I love design that is thought-provoking, intelligent or just downright beautiful. The problem is that I have limited access to this type of work, as I live in Indianapolis, not in a design capital. Being able to afford it is another issue. So, for people like me, if you have access to this book and a hardware store, you have access to some great designs.

Who will read – and make – *DIY Furniture*?
It's intended for anyone wanting well-designed, witty furnishings who is willing to put in the elbow grease in exchange for saving some money. The idea is to encourage non-makers to make things. Of the 30 projects in the book, some are easy and others require more patience. The materials are common: wood, tubing, rope, PVC pipe, concrete, zip ties – even a rubber doormat. The idea is that after making some of the objects in the book, the reader should have an arsenal of methods they can apply in making their own projects.

> *'I love design that is thought-provoking'*

In this age of 3D printing, why should we still use our hands?
I use 3D computer technology in my line of work and have no arguments against it. It's another way to self-produce in low volume and is great for smaller items like jewellery. It wouldn't be cost-effective, though, to make a large object like a chair using that technology. There is also a learning curve for those who don't know CAD. Anyway, as an artist I find it more gratifying to stick found objects together or to appropriate ready-made parts. It's immediate and more personal.

Why do a book and not, say, a website?
Call me old-fashioned, but there is something about a physical object. Besides, I seldom revisit sites, with the exception of design hubs that feature new content daily or social-media

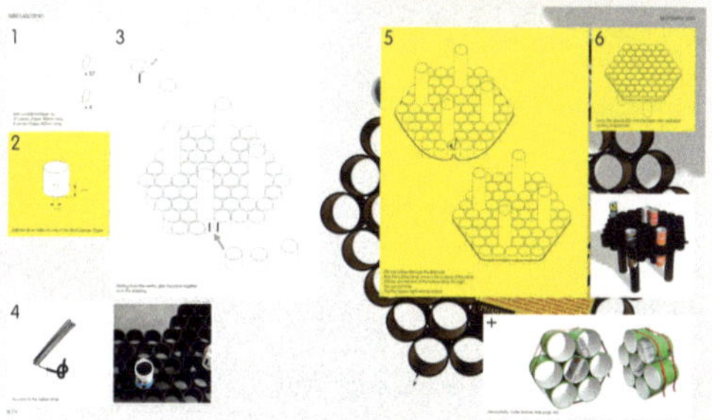

sites. I revisit my books and magazines and often read the same pages multiple times. I never throw them out.

What do you hope to achieve with *DIY Furniture*?
I hope that it will inspire people to be creative and that they will see, through creating, the value of good design, which should encourage them to take an interest in their design community.

Where else would you like to go with this project?
I like the idea of an exhibition, and I think the designs in the book are worthy of one. The work represents artists and designers of today who aren't just going with the grain. They are leaders and innovators who have blurred the line between art and design in response to a global economic shift and to mass production.

In an effort to create a community, we are also launching a Facebook page for the book, where people can go to learn more about the contributors, to ask questions, to share photos of their builds, and to get links to giveaways. You can find a link to the page on the Laurence King website. Finally, I have ideas for other books – starting perhaps with a *DIY Furniture Part 2*.

DIY Furniture
By Christopher Stuart
Laurence King Publishing
ISBN 978-1-85669-472-2

Next Issue
Frame 84
Jan/Feb 2012

Urban Legends

Next issue, *Frame* samples large-scale urban projects that strive for connectivity, community and communication. Clive Wilkinson's dazzling European headquarters for Macquarie Bank, Jean Nouvel's media-saturated, mini-metropolis of a department store in Milan, and Zaha Hadid's spectacular Wangjing Soho showroom – a taster for her mountainous new 'business community in Beijing' – offer vibrant variations on the city-within-a-city concept. Finally, we catch up with veteran designer and Pentagram-founder Kenneth Grange, whose designs have helped shape the urban landscape of London, before getting away from it all with the otherworldly art of Junya Ishigami.

Macquarie at Ropemaker, London, by Clive Wilkinson Architects.
Photo Riddle Stagg Photographers

SID LEE BOOT CAMP

For its first ever Boot Camp, Sid Lee Collective recruited eight multidisciplinary talents from across the globe to live and breathe creativity for 240 hours straight. Their mission? To reimagine the future of Fatboy®.

Words: Helen Savage
Design: Mélanie Boucher

'What we do at Sid Lee is not only about products or spaces; it's a full 360 brand experience'.

—Philippe Meunier

A CRASH COURSE IN CREATIVITY—The inaugural Sid Lee Collective Boot Camp—a Sid Lee Collective project sponsored by Autodesk and hosted in collaboration with Fatboy®, Autodesk and Frame magazine—was the brainchild of the agency's Creative Chief Philippe Meunier and Executive Creative Director Hélène Godin. The goal of the project wasn't to produce deliverable campaigns or products, but to immerse young creatives from different backgrounds and disciplines in Sid Lee's unique, no-boundaries creative process, an approach the agency calls Commercial Creativity™.

THE COACHES – Sid Lee's expert team of coaches was on hand to advise and guide the recruits throughout every stage of the Boot Camp.

(From left to right): Marie-Elaine Benoit – Creative Director; Hélène Godin – Creative Director and senior partner; Yann Mooney – Creative Director; Bertrand Cesvet – Chairman and senior partner; Kristoffer Ekman – Digital Experience Specialist; Vicky Chen – Strategist; Philippe Meunier – Creative Chief and senior partner; Martin LeBlanc – Architect and senior partner, Sid Lee Architecture

Photo: Yann Ostiguy (2M2); Photo assistant: Eldon Poncsak; Hair and make-up: Marco Marsolais (GLOSS)

A WONDER-FULLER life

THE MISSION — As soon as the recruits landed in Montreal, they were briefed on their 10-day mission: to take Dutch lifestyle brand Fatboy® into the next decade using the brand's slogan and philosophy, A Wonder-Fuller Life, as inspiration.

02

Sid Lee chose to partner with Fatboy® for the first ever Boot Camp because it shares with the agency an open, multidisciplinary approach perfect for this type of experimental project.

01 The EAT section comprised of a stripped-down linear kitchen with very basic amenities, decorated with Fatboy®'s Edison the Grand and Edison the Petit lights.

02 The PLAY area became a place for the campers to relax and interact with oversized Fatboy® cushions, beanbags and a huge hammock.

03 The REST area was the recruits' sleeping quarters, where they pitched army-style khaki tents with just a basic sleeping cot and small fan inside.

04 The MOVE section was the exercise area, complete with a punching bag, obstacle-course-style tyres, a swing and ladder, and yoga mats.

01

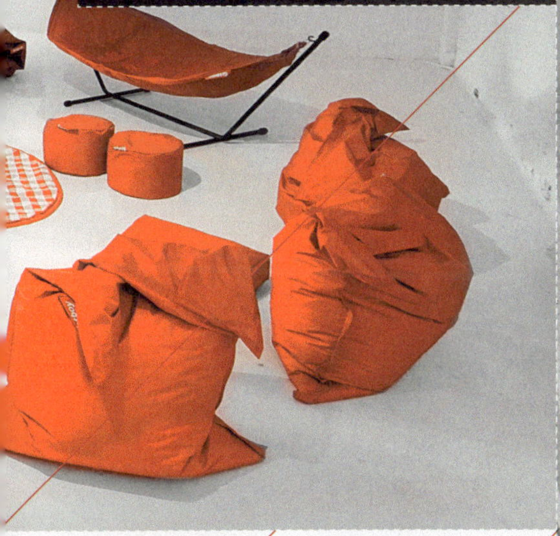

03

04

THE CAMP — For the next 240 hours, the recruits hunkered down in an industrial workspace, transformed into an indoor campground especially for the experience. The camp and the overall brief were divided into four sections — representing the themes of EAT, PLAY, REST and MOVE — and the Boot Camp team was asked to brainstorm about new Fatboy® products and experiences relating to each theme, to help people achieve *A Wonder-Fuller Life* when it comes to eating, playing, resting and moving.

'We were looking to create an experience that takes collaboration and creativity to a new level, à la Sid Lee, and we're thrilled that Fatboy® was up for the experiment.'

—Hélène Godin

01 A red lightning bolt marks the Boot Camp entrance at 8 Queen Street, Montreal (coincidentally representing the eight recruits).

02 A painted red carpet welcomes the recruits and leads to the Boot Camp Wall of Fame.

03 Cristiane Holzheid and the rest of the Boot Camp team share their ideas from the PLAY workshop with Hélène Godin.

THE DESIGN—The camp, conceived by Sid Lee and Sid Lee Architecture and produced by Hugues Letellier, was designed to be as clean and open as possible. The colour scheme is simple and minimalistic: black and white to represent Sid Lee and red for Fatboy®. The space was filled with Fatboy® products so that the recruits were constantly interacting with, and drawing inspiration from, the brand.

The recruits gathered every night around the makeshift campfire to bounce ideas and relax after an intensive day of creation. Photos: Elida Arrizza

Christiane Holzheid from Berlin in front of the Boot Camp Wall of Fame.

01 Sid Lee Strategist Vicky Chen and Fatboy® Brand Director Femke de Jonge brief the campers on the brand.

02 The campers organize their ideas for the EAT workshop.
Photos: Elida Arrizza

'We're here to reimagine the future of Fatboy® in a Wonder-Fuller way.'
—Vicky Chen

OPERATION: EAT

THE GUEST COACHES
Frédéric Gauthier—Co-founder and Editor, La Pastèque; Diane Bisson–Industrial Designer, Anthropologist

THE BRIEF—The temperature of the world is increasing every year, which is having a huge impact on the environment. For EAT, the recruits were asked to think of ways to capture heat and reuse it within the context of kitchens in the home.

MOBILIZING THE TROOPS—The intense Boot Camp itinerary included daily briefs, talks by industry experts, brainstorming sessions and early-morning exercise drills. But it wasn't all work and no play; the recruits enjoyed some well-deserved down time exploring the city of Montreal, taking part in all kinds of activities from taking a bike tour through the city to clowning around at the Cirque du Soleil HQ.

The campers dress up in skeleton costumes and cycle through Montreal for the city's annual Tour la Nuit bike event.
Photo: Mathieu Fortin

'Everybody had their own ideas and twists on the theme of PLAY and how it could relate to space, and that's what makes the whole process magical.'

—Martin Leblanc

OPERATION: PLAY

THE GUEST COACH
Martin Leblanc — Architect and senior partner, Sid Lee Architecture

THE BRIEF—The campers were asked to explore the theme of PLAY and how it could relate to space, challenging traditional notions of playful spaces for people of all ages.

01 Guest coach Martin Leblanc briefs the Boot Campers on the theme of PLAY.

02 The team researches new and innovative ways to approach PLAY.

03 The campers were asked to make their own models with "playful shapes".
Photos: Elida Arrizza

01

DAY 4 – 4:26 PM

02

'Sleep is the new sex.'
—Cristiane Bourbonnais

OPERATION: REST

THE GUEST COACH
Cristiane Bourbonnais—Owner, Cohesion Strategies

THE BRIEF—The theme of REST was broken down into three challenges: 1) Rest your body, exploring ways to help people enjoy a more restful sleep; 2) Rest your soul, examining the increasingly popular practice of house-swapping and couch-surfing and taking it to the next level; 3) Rest your cells, thinking about how we can shield the cells in our bodies from harmful energy (cell phones, microwaves, etc.)

The Boot Campers were working too hard to tidy their tents!

01 Cristiane Bourbonnais and the campers share their ideas from the REST workshop with Philippe Meunier and Hélène Godin.

02 The recruits write their ideas on Post-its and stick them on the creative wall for inspiration, a common practice at Sid Lee.
Photos: Elida Arrizza

Jonas Johansson empties the contents of a Fatboy® beanbag over campmate Stéphanie Lebœuf
Photo: Elida Arrizza

01 It's raining Fatboy®: the team makes a splash with a fan and Styrofoam balls. Photo: Elida Arrizza

02 MOVE coach Lucy McRae takes a load off on Jonas Johansson's Fatboy® suit. Photo: Elida Arrizza

03 Camp Chief Kristoffer Ekman and Boot Camper Albane Guy bury themselves in the Fatboy® "floor". Photo: Lucy McRae

01

'We asked everyone to climb inside empty Fatboy® products, to escape from the regular world into the Wonder-Fuller world.'

—Lucy McRae

OPERATION: MOVE

THE GUEST COACH
Lucy McRae—artist, body architect, dancer

THE BRIEF—The challenge for MOVE was to explore the human body in relation to the surrounding environment, and to deconstruct Fatboy® products to experience them from a different perspective.

02

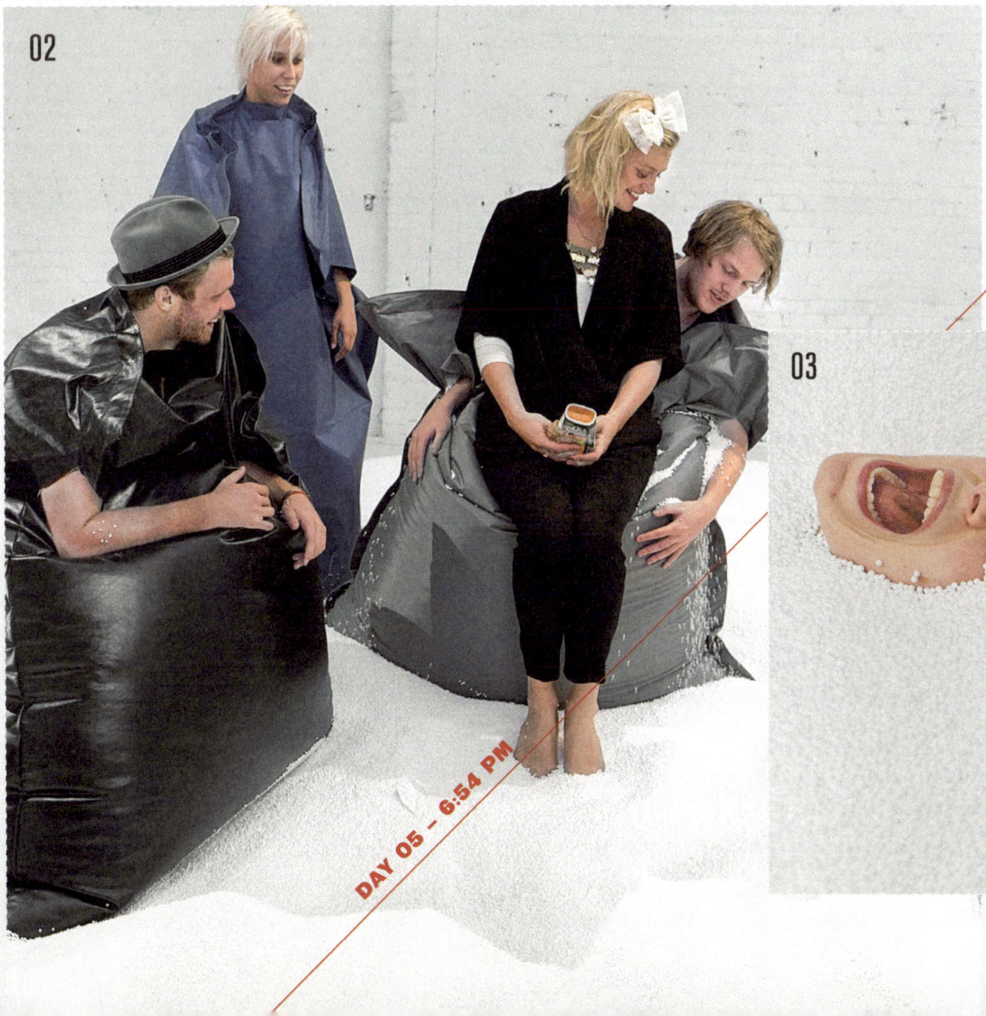

DAY 05 – 6:54 PM

03

PLAY
01
02

The campers take turns diving through a paper wall onto a makeshift Fatboy® floor.
Photos: Yann Ostiguy (2M2)

01 The campers form a train with oversized Fatboy® pillows.

02 The recruits use their bodies and Fatboy® products to make a giant red and white flower.

Sid Lee Chairman and senior partner Bertrand Cesvet steps in to "shake up the troops" halfway through the Boot Camp, while coaches Yann Mooney and Philippe Meunier look on.

01 The campers present their ideas so far to the Sid Lee team.

02 The team works through the night to finalize their ideas from the Boot Camp.

03 Kristoffer Ekman and campers Bauke Knottnerus and Jonas Johansson work on their idea of floating tents for *A Wonder-Fuller Land* (see pages 30-31).
Photos: Elida Arrizza

01

'At this stage [day five] they fall in love with their ideas and it takes someone external to come in and say, "Is that really a good idea?"'

—Bertrand Cesvet

02

03

The recruits are woken up at the crack of dawn to go for a run around Montreal's Old Port.
Photo: Mathieu Fortin

'We wanted people with talent and edge. Because we do a lot of recruitment at schools around the world, I think we have the touch when it comes to finding people who can work well together.'

—Hélène Godin

SID LEE WANTS YOU!—Following a hugely successful online recruitment campaign, Sid Lee received hundreds of applications from Boot Camp hopefuls hailing from more than 25 countries around the world. After a rigorous screening process, the final eight were selected based not only on their portfolios but also on their personalities and how Meunier and Godin felt they would contribute to the group dynamic.

DAY 3 – 7:08 AM

The campers take a breather after tackling the Boot Camp obstacle course.
Photo: Mathieu Fortin

Kristoffer Ekman, a Digital Experience Specialist at Sid Lee, was in charge of helping the troops come together as a team. He lived with them for the entire Boot Camp.

Photos: Neil Mota (L'Éloi)
Art Director: Mélanie Boucher
Creative Associate: Loc
Photo Assistant: Enrique Sanchez
Stylist: Sara Bruneau (Satellite)
Hair and make-up: Maïna Militza (Satellite)
Hair and make-up photographer: Christopher Dormoy

'It was work hard, play hard.'

—Kristoffer Ekman

All of the recruits come from a multidisciplinary background and contributed equally to every aspect of the creative process during the Boot Camp, stepping out of their comfort zones and crossing creative borders.

STÉPHANIE LEBOEUF
Canada

ARCHITECT

'It was an amazing experience and interesting to see such a different creative approach.'

Intern at Sid Lee architecture / Born and raised in Montreal / Studied architecture at the Université de Montréal / Passionate about urban planning and exploring the dichotomy between man-made and natural landscapes

ART DIRECTOR / GRAPHIC DESIGNER

'Now it's over, I feel overwhelmed, humbled, and excited for what's coming next.'

Newly hired as an art director at Sid Lee / Originally from Antwerp, Belgium / Studied graphic design in Belgium and Athens, Greece / Portfolio includes work for Diesel, eBoy and Ed Fella

ROEBEN BEDDELEEM
Belgium

BAUKE KNOTTNERUS
Netherlands

ART DIRECTOR/MATERIAL DESIGNER

'The creative process was so fluid because of the strong grid Sid Lee put in place.'

Owns a design studio in Rotterdam, Netherlands / Born and raised in Rotterdam / Graduate of the Design Academy in Eindhoven, Netherlands / Merging industrial and furniture design with a passion for fashion, he is fascinated by scale and using basic stylistic ideas with new proportions

COPYWRITER

'The highlights for me were interacting with different disciplines in a creative framework. To be surrounded by that calibre of people, you learn so much.'

Copywriter at Wieden + Kennedy in Portland, Oregon / Born and raised in Milwaukee, Wisconsin / Master's degree in copywriting from VCU Brandcenter, Virginia / Interned at Saatchi & Saatchi L.A. / Has worked for clients including Prius, Nascar and Toyota Rebrand

SAMUEL DOLPHIN
United States

CHRISTIANE HOLZHEID

Germany

CREATIVE TECHNOLOGIST / MEDIA DESIGNER

'The first few days, we were really taken out of our comfort zones to get us in a creative mindset.'

Freelance Media Designer in Berlin, Germany / Originally from Coburg, Germany / Master's in media design from the Art Center College of Design in Pasadena, California / Passionate about storytelling and social media, she believes hybrid thinking is the key to great design

CREATIVE TECHNOLOGIST / ART DIRECTOR

'Nobody ever lost intensity or energy. That was the most inspiring part of this experience for me.'

Interactive Art Director at Weiden + Kennedy, Tokyo / Originally from Glommen, Sweden / Graduate of Hyper Island's Interactive Art Director program / Comfortable working in multiple creative roles, he strives never to repeat himself in his work

JONAS JOHANSSON

Sweden

ENVIRONMENTAL DESIGNER

'It was very open, very creative, and it's been emotional. I'm really sad it's over.'

Freelance designer in Montreal / Originally from Lyon, France / Studied event design at the Université du Québec à Montréal / Has freelanced on a diverse range of projects including event design for Renzo Design and scenography for the International Literature Festival

SANJA DEVRIES, GRAPHIC DESIGNER

'I came here as a graphic designer, unsure of what my role would be. But we all really came together and crossed borders.'

Studying graphic design at the Willem de Kooning Academie, Rotterdam, Netherlands / Interned at Dutch ad agency NEROC'VGM and Rabobank Nederland / Has freelanced for clients including North Sea Jazz and La deuxième vie / Passionate about beautiful design in all its forms

A WONDER-FULLER land

The recruits worked through the night to produce an impressive Sid Lee roll, the culmination of their creative ideas from the 10-day Boot Camp.

01 Material designer Bauke Knottnerus developed a proposed Fatboy® texture series featuring playful products like this, the Furry Boy.

02 A mock-up of the floating tents from *A Wonder-Fuller Land.*

03 The campers present their roll to the Fatboy® clients and Sid Lee team.
Photos: Elida Arrizza

01

MISSION ACCOMPLISHED—After an intense and exhausting 10 days, the Boot Camp team presented their ideas in an impressive Sid Lee roll. Tasked with creating innovative and immersive Fatboy experiences, the final result was *A Wonder-Fuller Land*—a living art installation complete with floating cocoon-like tents where guests are invited to create their own light, colour and sound orchestrations.

Sid Lee was overwhelmed by the unprecedented success of its first Boot Camp and the positive response it drew from people across the globe. The agency now plans to host Boot Camps at least once a year, offering different brands an opportunity to benefit from a unique creative process that produces ground-breaking ideas with great marketing potential... and to spread the message of collaborative creativity one Boot Camp at a time!

02

03

Sanja Devries signs her Boot Camp "uniform" before flying back home to Holland. Photo: Elida Arrizza

Check out all the photos and videos from the Boot Camp at:

http://vimeo.com/channels/sidleebootcamp2011
http://j.mp/SIDCAMPpix
http://www.facebook.com/MeetSidLee

SID LEE COLLECTIVE WOULD LIKE TO THANK ITS SPONSOR, AUTODESK—ALONG WITH ITS TRUSTED PARTNERS, FATBOY® AND FRAME MAGAZINE—FOR THEIR SUPPORT AND COLLABORATION IN MAKING THIS PROJECT HAPPEN. WE WOULD ALSO LIKE TO THANK EVERYONE AT SID LEE, SID LEE ARCHITECTURE AND JIMMY LEE WHO GOT INVOLVED TO HELP MAKE SID LEE'S FIRST EVER BOOT CAMP A TRULY UNFORGETTABLE EXPERIENCE.

SID LEE Collective fatboy FRAME Autodesk